Lenox Staring At The Ceiling

by J. Jube

CITI OF BOOKS

CITIOFBOOKS, INC.
3736 Eubank NE Suite A1
Albuquerque, NM 87111-3579
www.citiofbooks.com
Hotline: 1 (877) 389-2759
Fax: 1 (505) 930-7244

Ordering Information:
Quantity sales. Special discounts are available on quantity purchases by corporations, associations, and others. For details, contact the publisher at the address above.

Printed in the United States of America.

ISBN-13:	Softcover	979-8-89391-448-1
	eBook	979-8-89391-447-4

Library of Congress Control Number: 2024924763

Table of Contents

I believe that the only way relationships survive and thrive is by being completely vulnerable and accepting that the path forward in life is always filled with obstacles and challenges and the process is where life happens. We should never shy away from being uncomfortable even when the road ahead isn't as clear as we'd like it to be. Pain, uncertainty, and constant growth will always be the cornerstones of our reality and we must embrace and cherish them, and be grateful, forgiven, and curious, for without them, we are only but an empty shell.

"Life is what happens when you are busy making other plans." (John Lennon - Beautiful Boy).

Prologue

I have had in the back of my mind for many years that I want to be a writer, an actor, a musician, or someone with a message that people would enjoy listening, watching, hearing about it. But then, something would always stop me on my tracks; perhaps the fear that nobody would read or listen to what I have to say and the prospect that nobody would care frightened me beyond my courage to get up and do it. Again, the familiar voice would persist; "you can't do it, you know you can't do it, why would your story be relevant or interesting?" A confusion and a sense of unimportance and irrelevance would prevail to win out every time I thought about putting pen to paper and I'd keep on pushing it to the side, looking for distractions and mostly just keeping it as a distant objective for some other time in the future, not now, sort of like an unattained goal which could only exist in my incessant state of daydreaming while staring at the ceiling, hence the title of this book.

My dreams have always ran wild and my curiosity to explore the experience of writing, to be read, to be heard and watched would only last for a few minutes before I find something to derail me from getting to work on it and diving into the process of allowing myself to be vulnerable, to embrace and welcome the twists and turns of writing without hesitation or constraints by pouring myself into this journey and transform it into an exciting and appealing good read, if for nobody else, at least for me.

I often hear some of my favorite musicians and artists speak about their creative process and it's often said that you must create for yourself, because you like it and because it has a meaning to the creator, because it's honest and genuine even when it's about dishonesty. There's no one else like you in this whole universe and that should be a good enough reason to do it. Perhaps others will like it too or relate to it, or even better; be inspired by it and put their own pen to paper and find their voices while losing themselves in the vulnerable meandering of writing.

I am well aware that writing is hard work, a form of catharsis, and I am writing because I want to own my shortcomings and change the narrative of my life going forward with the hopes to inspiring people I love the most; my children and a handful of other people who perhaps will read this and hopefully break the cycles, the modes, the dogmas and conditioning we learn from early on, or perhaps just have a good laugh or a well deserved cry.

Although cleansing one's heart and mind can be rather painful, I believe to be worthwhile and courageous all at once, after all, who hasn't made life altering mistakes which in many instances kept us from moving forward and being the best version of ourselves? I know I have, and I wouldn't change a thing.

Dedication

Something inspired me on March 8, 2020 and I am taking a leap of faith to change these few minutes of daydreaming and desire to write and transform this abstract and far out dream into something palpable, into a reality, into a project right in the middle of a pandemic on top of the most beautiful treehouse ever built, The Mahina Treehouse. I am taking the leap of faith and diving into my piece of art, my "Mona Lisa" of sorts which I am certain will keep me in touch with my inner self, with my struggles, with my strengths but specially with my vulnerabilities and weaknesses.

I spent my entire Sunday morning on March 8, 2020, at Jane's garden in the company of my daughter Isabela, my nephew Luka, Jane and our little pooch Bebe which we share since Jane and I got divorced in May of 2015. I noticed all the beautiful flowers, trees and the smell of nature which made me think that I have it in me, I have a gift of a life well lived and a life that only a few people get the opportunity to experience. When I looked at Jane and Isabela that Sunday morning, I got inspired because they are without a doubt the most beautiful people in the world and the love of my life along with my other two children Victor and Noah. So, I decided to come home, climb up to the Mahina Treehouse where I have been living while still under construction for the last six years, open my computer and get started and hopefully not stop until I empty my heart, my mind, and my soul. It doesn't matter how long it takes, it doesn't matter what the little voices over my shoulders whine about and try to convince me otherwise. I won't stop until I get to accomplish the task at hand; write a book not just about my experiences lived but also about my dreams, the ever-elusive big dreams of mine.

My mind and those annoying voices are already fucking with me however and making me feel a bit arrogant and pretentious when I say "write a book" because I have so much admiration and respect for writers and artists in general that to put me in the same category feels like an insult to them. "You are not your thoughts Lenox, snap the fuck out of it," I keep on reminding myself.

Every good writer and artist must've taken a leap of faith to overcome their fears and the notion that nobody is paying attention and must've taken the plunge into the abyss, why not me? Still, the fear of not being relevant persists and I am fighting it in every stroke on the keyboard but the feeling of "dude, who the fuck you think you are?" persists in the back of my head and it's a constant fight. Well, I am deciding not to listen to it, not to pay attention to the thousands of insane, discombobulated self-doubt thoughts that insist and persist in telling me I am not good enough, not important, or relevant enough, but you know what? Fuck my fifty thousand plus disjointed daily thoughts...I am forging ahead, with or without my approval, because as one of my heroes once said and I'm paraphrasing here: "The thrill is in the journey and not on the goal or the accomplishment itself."

I have been considering this idea for a long time, in fact, in the last 30 years and hundreds of long journeys in cramped American Airlines planes, I have written six filled journals/diaries and the thought of putting my life in a concise and chronological order have always been attractive to me. At first glance, it seemed simple from the point of organizing my thoughts but I know my thoughts are complicated and intertwined with feelings and therefore the simplicity I naively imagine, can be a daunting task. The inspiration to go home and get started however, was triggered not only by the beautiful garden and nature, but also by Jane and Isabela, who were there with me that day and are the most influential women in my life and the people who changed how I see the world, how I behave, how I act, how I love and navigate thru this miracle thing called life. They have shown me that love and passion, hard work, perseverance, patience, kindness, softness, fairness, honesty, openness, vulnerability, hard work, transparency, subtleness, grit and beauty in every way, shape and form can be a transforming recipe for someone as lost as I was and have been since childhood. I hope that whoever reads this book gets just as inspired, if not to the extent of opening their computer and spilling their hearts and souls into it, perhaps to change their own lives, to break some of the vicious cycles and conditionings and forge ahead with a purpose, with passion and a desire that resides in all of us but is often hidden within the layers of complicated thoughts, early patterns, erratic behaviors, and vicious cycles we learn as children. Layers of disjointed feelings which gets us confused for who we are - definitely not our thoughts - feelings that we learn to attach to our existence as if we identify ourselves through them. Feelings, and conditionings that we learn throughout and if not understood and dealt with, stay with us and spill over to our children repeating the same chain of transgenerational trauma while depriving us of a life well lived in this short time we have on earth.

This book is specially dedicated to my beautiful and amazing children and greatest inspiration; Victor, Isabela and Noah, and the reason I live my life with such vigor and passion and in the present, with unconstrained joy in every moment and every breath I take. To Jane, whom I've always love unconditionally and is someone whom I've learned the meaning of love, kindness, and generosity. To my loving sisters and passionate brothers who never ceased to encourage, motivate, and inspire me with their unconditional love and support. To my late mom and dad who sacrificed their own lives just to have me as part of their journey. It's also dedicated to all the unsung heroes who one way or another inspire me daily, knowingly or unknowingly to have the courage to follow my bliss and become a better man than I have been taught to be, the dream of becoming a writer, an artist, people who go thru the arduous process of creative writing and art; albeit a song, an essay, a short story, a poem, a painting, a book about anything, especially when it is about our lives and all the vulnerability that encompasses a genuine heartfelt story. Afterall, isn't great art always a reflection of the artist's life struggles and the reason we feel connected to it?

I expect this process to be therapeutic at least and humbling at most.

Acknowledgement

I would like to acknowledge and express my gratitude to Jullia Finkelstein, without whom the cover of this book would've never come to existence. Thank you for your patience with my ever annoying and endless phone calls and text messages. Your talents, skills, kindness, and attention to details are an inspiration to me.

In Memoriam

"When you're in the mountains, with a mission, it's like all of the superficialities of life just sort of evaporate, and you can often find yourself in a deeper state of mind, and that can stick with you for a while after a big climb. You appreciate everything so much, that you take for granted most of the time. It's kind of funny. The actual achievement doesn't really change your life, like you think it might, but what you're left with is the journey that got you to that point."

Marc-Andre LeClerc – Alpinist

CHAPTER I

The Shoes Under the Table

That hot and dry summer of 1970 I had just turned five years old a few months prior, and my memory hadn't always served me as well as I would like it to, but I remember being pushed around the yard in a red wooden fire truck by my cousin Isabel Maria who happened to be a few years older than me. The red wooden fire truck was a gift from my father who would come home from his long working journeys and often brought me wooden truck toys he would usually find in small stands along the side of the roads where he would stop to rest a little, have a shot of cachaça and smoke his beloved Hollywood cigarettes while stretching his legs during the long working trips he often took as a truck and cab driver in order to support his five kids and his wife.

My father was in many ways a "do it all" kind of man. He was a mechanic, a taxi and truck driver by necessity, a husband by accident, and I am sure a father by default and pure stubbornness. As a young boy I thought that my father was the epitome of manhood, however. His wavy and slick hair, his deep penetrating blue eyes, his angular and strong facial expressions, his slim and incredibly nimble strong body, his unmistakably macho man persona, his dark and thick mustache, and his never-ending energy and brute strength made me believe that to be a man, that's how I needed to be. I wanted to emulate everything my father portrayed except that I didn't know if I had the patience to be a mechanic, the skill set to be a great driver like my old man, the need to become a husband and the desire to be a father. In other words, I didn't have any of the attributes and traits he had, I thought.

Jose Simao Ramos Jube, that's his entire name. A man who at the age of two lost his own father to a heart condition and with his young single mother, his two half-brothers Jordelino and Sebastiao, and his two sisters Laila and Ana, had to find a way to survive in the world without a father, a penny to their names and a place to call home. My father had this clear and lucid memory however, which to this day I wonder if he actually remembered from the age of two all the stories he'd tell us with such details till the day he died just a few years back, or if he just had a very creative imagination because he would go into such minutiae and so far back that I could not understand how anyone could remember his entire life inside out from such a young age all the way to 84 when he passed. His memory was impeccable and incredibly clear. He would recall adventurous tales of how he would ride the neighbors horses at the age of three and all the places he would go with his two older brothers to find food, mostly consisting of someone else's chickens and pigs they'd steal and bring home, kill it, clean it, and present it to his mother for their one meal a day menu which would consist of chicken or pig stew, white rice cooked in the only copper pan they had with sautéed garlic, onions, salt and pepper. The family would have each of their meal with a piece of old stale bread, which would hold them off for the entire day. Some neighbor farmers who felt sorry for the extreme poverty to which they lived under would give my grandmother; Messias Silva Rosa, the rice grains and whatever else they didn't want it anymore. They would eat a small portion of their daily findings once a day around 3pm so it would cover lunch and dinner and save every scrap and every left over for the next day. My father's mom would pick some old stale left over bread from church after Sunday's mass near where they lived and that was their breakfast whenever they were lucky enough to get their hand on the old loaf of bread. Life was difficult and there was no time to ponder or dream about anything since the only order of the day was to survive, to gather whatever scraps of food they could find and keep shelter at the old, moldy, dark, cold, and cramped basement behind the village church where my grandmother would pray three times a day for better days. I often wonder how could you not survive and thrive when you pray that much? I guess God can't ignore such persistence, and neglect so much misery, can he? Yes, he can!!!

So, I grew up with these stories in my memory, with the picture of these desperate kids roaming around in search of food. The noise of the chickens flapping their wings trying to escape their capturers, the squealing of the pigs being stolen and killed with a sharp metal thrusting thru their heart and being dissected for cooking oil and meat, feet, ears, skin, and every eatable and non-eatable part of their carcasses on salt drying in the sun for a future meal. To this day, from telling, listening, and writing about those stories, I can feel the texture of the stale bread in my mouth and the sweetness of garlic and onions aroma jumping on the copper pan mixed with the washed rice and water retrieved from the water well behind the church in an aluminum bucket with so many holes in it which by the time it got to the top of the well it was already half full, I lived that childhood thru my father's beautiful stories. These noises and tastes were not always my experiences, but they became part of me and later, eventually repeated themselves in my own up bringing, like many other things repeated themselves over, and over again. These noises and tastes and aromas were ingrained in my soul and in my spirit besides being impregnated in my senses and my memory.

Later in life I grew up with the noise of the burning of the cachaça in my father's throat as he'd sip on it three times a day religiously; before he went to work, when he would come home for lunch and before supper. God only knows how many more sips of cachaça he'd taken throughout his day. I never thought of my father as an alcoholic and never considered him to be a man of many vices or addictions although I knew he always smoke two packs of Hollywood's a day, drank his liquor often and even offered the left over to the gods as he called it and had an expert set of blue eyes for any skirt who walked by. I never gave too much thought to how much a parent could influence their children until I became a father myself but by then, the damaged was already done. I was doomed.

I can't explain how I was raised because I don't think I was. I was given a life and had to do the raising part of it on my own by watching my father do his, monkey see monkey do style. I learned by watching my father treat his wives the same way he learned how from his own father, his older half-brother Jordelino, his taxi driver friends, and his macho men mechanic colleagues. I don't think I had a learning experience from my father but rather, I simply repeated some of the same behaviors which have paved a long and rough road thru life which somehow, and in some strange ways got me here.

For better or for worse, I made this far and had I only repeated what I have witnessed, I don't believe I would be here to write about it today. So, I digress and admit I must have learned a few good things along the way from my old man, intentionally or not and had some good examples as well because I didn't turn out too bad of a person, that of course will depend on who you ask I suppose, some folks might have something to say about that!

On that June 3, 1970, while parked inside my wooden fire truck under that strange table in our living room, I thought it was strange to have so many people in our house. I lived in this poor neighborhood called Vila Nova in Goiania, a city in the middle of Brazil, about 200 kilometers from the Brazilian capital, Brasilia. Goiania is one of these towns where there's nothing interesting about it except it was where my family lived. I'd always dreamt about running away from that hot, dusty, humid, uninspired, and weird city. The house where we lived was still there just a few months before I started to write this book. We sold it to a stranger and plenty of our history got lost with it. It was a three bedroom and one very small bathroom, a cramped kitchen a TV room with black and red patterned cold ceramic tiles, a small living room with an old Essenfelder piano where my older sister Marina first learned how to play and later taught lessons to put herself thru medical school and help with the expenses. The bedrooms were miniscule, and the brick and plastered walls had mold from water which always penetrated thru the roof, old age and dents from the furniture throwing that it would take place more often than I'd care to remember. The bathroom was a small square room with a blue toilet without a toilet seat or cover, the walls had blue ceramic tiles from the floor all the way to the ceiling. The shower was an electric piece of engineering put together by my father with the wires all exposed and the water would run either too hot or too cold and it didn't have enough water pressure, but we couldn't dare to touch the "summer/winter" switch because we would be zapped and electrocuted in the process. Occasionally friends would come to visit, and we'd would forget to tell them not to touch the shower head, and without an exception, they all got zapped by that fucking shower head and I'd only remember to tell them after hearing the screaming and they'd be terrified because it was a strong current and the power would go off in the entire house.

I often thought that perhaps my father wired that shower head in such a way with the hopes to eliminate some of us to ease the load because I honestly don't know how anyone could survive that electric current with water falling over their heads just as much as I always thought that there were too many of us and some of us wouldn't survive our living conditions. The blue sink in the bathroom had a flimsy small plastic medicine cabinet and a cracked mirror which we could hide our worn-out toothbrushes from gigantic cockroaches and any potential guest who might come to our house. In the medicine cabinet there was also a plastic rolled up tube of Colgate which we had to do magic quite often to get anything out of it, my father's rusted and dull Gillette razor blades in a match box and his razor which would get a rusty and dulled razor blade every two months or so. There we could also find a bottle of Johnson oil, my father's favorite hair conditioner which he used daily on his hair and combed from front to back with his old plastic Flamengo comb he always kept on his jeans right back pocket. There was no shower curtain to speak of and in Brazil we don't throw toilet paper inside the toilet unless we wanted to clog the entire pluming system, so all the rubbish went into an old and rusty aluminum basket without a plastic bag I might add, which we kept in the corner to the right of the toilet bowl. Needless to say that small rubbish basket had to be emptied several times daily with so many people and one tiny bathroom for all of us.

The boys bedroom - there were two boys till I was 8 years old and five boys thereafter - barely fit one bed so in later years we managed to fit two tiny bunk beds, one on each side and one thin mattress in the middle where my oldest sister Marina slept because the girl's bedroom was even smaller and only had two very small twin size beds in it, a small dresser and an old wooden closet where everyone kept their clothes and shared four small drawers which never really slid open easily and had to be yanked to the point that the whole closet would shake and lean forward almost falling on top of us when trying to open the drawers. In one of those drawers, my sister Marina would keep a can of Nestle condensed milk, which was her sweet treat, no wonder she struggles with her sugar intake and diabetes later in life. She would punch two holes with a sharp knife on top of the can and would hide it under her panties so nobody could touch it, especially the ants…except for the always hungry and curious me who snooped around looking for candy and any kind of food around the house. Both bedrooms had glass window louvers, which were so old and rusted we never bothered to close them because we wouldn't be able to open them at night when we were at the mercy of the Goiania's heat and the noisy mosquitos buzzing in our ears all night long as we struggle to fall asleep. Some nights we would be hitting our heads and ears to kill the mosquitos prompting my father to spray the entire house with his hand pump and a deadly Bayer mosquito killer which not only killed the mosquitos but made us dizzy and gave us headaches because it was very poisonous and lethal to any living thing. No wonder we are all fucked up in some corky ways and certainly we still suffer from breathing that stuff, again, supporting my theory that my father was always looking for ways to get rid of some of us hoping only the strong would survive… shit we all survived, and in my view the Bayer spray was another method of weeding out the weak ones. There was no master bedroom to speak of, but rather my father and my mother and later my stepmother had a full size bed which barely fit them, a mosquito net hanging from the ceiling which was pure luxury, a three door falling apart closet and a dresser with two drawers that wouldn't slide open, a rusted and cracked on the right side corner rectangular mirror and two night stands without lamps where my father kept his 22 caliber Beretta revolver, his old and mostly non-operational hand tools which he used on the weekends to fix his boss's 1966 VW TL, some nuts and bolts he would bring back from this mechanic shop he worked at a few times during the week, and his wallet which was fat and gigantic and overfilled with receipts, small notes and a few bucks. He never knew how much he had in his wallet or pocket, perhaps because he never had enough and there was no point in counting. My father had so much crap that he would use his and my mother's drawers leaving her with no space for her trinkets…don't you dare challenge his drawer space, it was his and his alone, just like the entire house was and we were just visitors there, purely passengers on a road to nowhere.

The living room had an old and broken couch which was covered with a blanket to hide all the holes and pieces of foam oozing out of its old raggedy covers. We would all fight for a corner in it to watch whatever one of the three channels my father would be able to scrounge by going up on the rooftop of the house and manage to put some aluminum foil or BOMBRIL on the tip of the broken rusted and busted into five pieces old umbrella he figured as a TV antenna. Who cares about remote controls when you only have three channels and the only decent show a kid could watch was Tom & Jerry once a week on Wednesday at 6:05 PM right after the daily Ave Maria prayer at 6 PM. The rest were Brazilian novelas (soup operas), which was too improper for anyone half intelligent to watch and still is. Yet, we would sit there and breathe the Bayer mosquito spray and indulge the Ave Maria every evening and sometimes cry out of desperation, out of hunger, out of hopelessness, out of fear of what the future would look like for us, or at least I did. I'd always quietly and privately wondered about our future, and it scared me shitless to have to live that way forever. Discussing or talking about anything in our house, sharing your thoughts, having a conversation, and questioning anything and asking why or how about anything was strictly prohibited and usually heavily punished. It was intimidating and terrifying for not being able to say anything, to have a voice or give an opinion or to request a different channel or have second servings on the left-over soup made from scraps from lunch. That type of wondering, sadness and desperation became a way of living to me. Suddenly it becomes all you know and morphs into normalcy to feel lost, depressed, hungry, anxious, angry, and sad and we were just a bunch of little kids trying to raise themselves..

That type of upbringing would often bring me to tears then, and it brings me to tears now because the smell of mold, Bayer mosquito spray, bean soup, the hot oil in the air from the fried egg my dad would have on his bowl of soup (we didn't have eggs for everyone) would make me want to disappear and question why the fuck was I there? In fact, I questioned many times why I was put on this planet? What right my parents had to keep having one kid after another while my mother was ill, weak, frail, and dying? Nothing made any sense to me, and I can't imagine that it ever made any sense to them, but again, they seemed not to know any better or just didn't care and kept popping up one baby after another like rabbits do, except as far as I know, rabbits don't fuck their pups up.

The kitchen had one small table that would fit maybe four people because one side of it was against the wall so it would fit in the cramped space. There was a cockroach infested blue aluminum cabinet where plates, utensils and food supplies could be found. The doors had a magnetic system which would never work properly for they were flimsy, crooked, and falling apart and the magnets never really lined up and never worked. On top of the cabinet there were containers with sugar, salt, with spices, a few matchboxes for my father's smoking enjoyment and to light up the also blue and falling into pieces four burner gas stove. In the middle of the cabinet there were two broken sliding acrylic doors where the small glass cups, mugs and plates would be kept and the entire cabinet was just filled with rust, big and small roaches, which were by this time, unliked us kids, happy permanent residents and resistant to the Bayer bug spray. The cabinet seemed clean to our standards however, that's all we knew. On the left-hand side next to the TODDY chocolate powder there was a bottle of "51 Cachaça," a deadly 39.9% alcohol content time bomb beauty that you could run your automobile on it, which in some instances my dad would pour it in the carburetor of the VW in the morning to get it started. My father would hit that bottle three times a day religiously, like clockwork, we might not have enough milk, in fact we never had milk but rather drank Matte but the old 51 cachaça bottle was always there, just like the fucking roaches, another permanent resident and a loyal partner of my father and his Gods.

In the back yard there were two mango trees where I would climb during mango season and pick mangos to sell at recess time at the schools nearby to have money for shoes and socks. It was hard to wear my sister's shoes and have my toes all cramped and hurting from the pair of white Congas two sizes too small we share amongst ourselves. My favorite tree however was our old guava tree where I would climb daily not only to eat the fresh pink guavas but to contemplate about my next move, my dreams and which pick-up truck I was going to purchase after I leave home and make some money. Which city one day I would escape to and never come back to this dreaded place? Which woman I'd find along the way that could give me a sense of family and motherly love, which I never had? I would spend all my afternoons up on the guava tree since school was from 7:30 AM to noon Monday to Friday and the afternoons were free to dream except for the chores like a bathroom to wash with buckets of water and Kiboa (Clorox) from top to bottom or a backyard to sweep with all the fruit tree leaves that dropped daily.

I would spend most of my free time up on the guava tree, watching people pass by under the branches hanging over the cracked and broken sidewalk. I'd hear their giggling and fights and the bullying from the bigger and stronger kids who constantly beat me up and made fun of my skinny and tall frame. Sometimes I'd witness the kids who lived down the street laughing of happiness and relief to be walking home from school after spending all afternoon in a hot and ran down classroom without air conditioner or proper ventilation. Thank God they never knew I was up there listening and watching them, those mean fuckers would shake me off the guava tree and I was so high up that they wouldn't even have to worry about finishing the job, I would simply explode on contact on the cracked sidewalk like the over ripped guavas did when they fell. Their school was just around the corner from our house, and I could see it from the top of the tree. I would watch and hear the cars with their rusted and broken mufflers zooming by our corner lot and the ice pop man pushing his little cart screaming: "orange, tangerine, coconut, get one and you will find happiness." I never had money to get one, so happiness never came!

I often wonder when I would be able to learn how to drive and have my own automobile and drive away from that place and never look back. I promised myself that I'd never drive with a rusted and broken muffler because we couldn't hear the 6:00 PM Ave Maria prayer on tv and listen to the sounds of Tom & Jerry cartoon when the cars passed by, even though there was no dialog between Tom & Jerry characters, I still wanted to hear the sounds of it but it was impossible when the old Vespas and the old cars zoomed by our corner house shaking every glass door and window in the house like a fucking 8.5 earthquake on the Richter scale. The challenge was that if we closed the small wooden front door, and the rusted and heavy living room window, we would suffocate with the Bayer spray and the heat, if we left it open, we couldn't hear a thing, what a clusterfuck! Goiania's climate is dry and dusty, and the heat is very intense for any living creature to handle, except those noisy blood sucking mosquitos, and the permanent resident kitchen cabinet roaches. I don't think I ever missed Goiania after I left and honestly, I don't think anybody would.

That June 3rd 1970 felt rather different and strange though. There were so many people in our home; uncles and aunties, cousins, familiar and unfamiliar faces in a very serious, somber, and sad mood, walking into and around the house while I was being pushed around on the red wooden truck toy by my cousin Isabela Maria. She pushed me in the backyard till we had to go somewhere else. Then she pushed me on the cracked sidewalk around all the cars parked in front of our house, and I would admire all the fancy (to me any car was fancy) VWs, Fords,

Chevys and all the different models and I'd remember of the time when my mother was in a hospital and I would go to the window and tell her the brand of each of the cars approaching the stop light near the hospital and I could tell her by the sound of it if it was a 1966 VW TL or a 1969 FORD Corcel. My ability to tell the difference and how often I was correct would impress her and made me super proud of myself.

She later while in a hospital bed where she spent most of her adult life wrote me a letter about that.

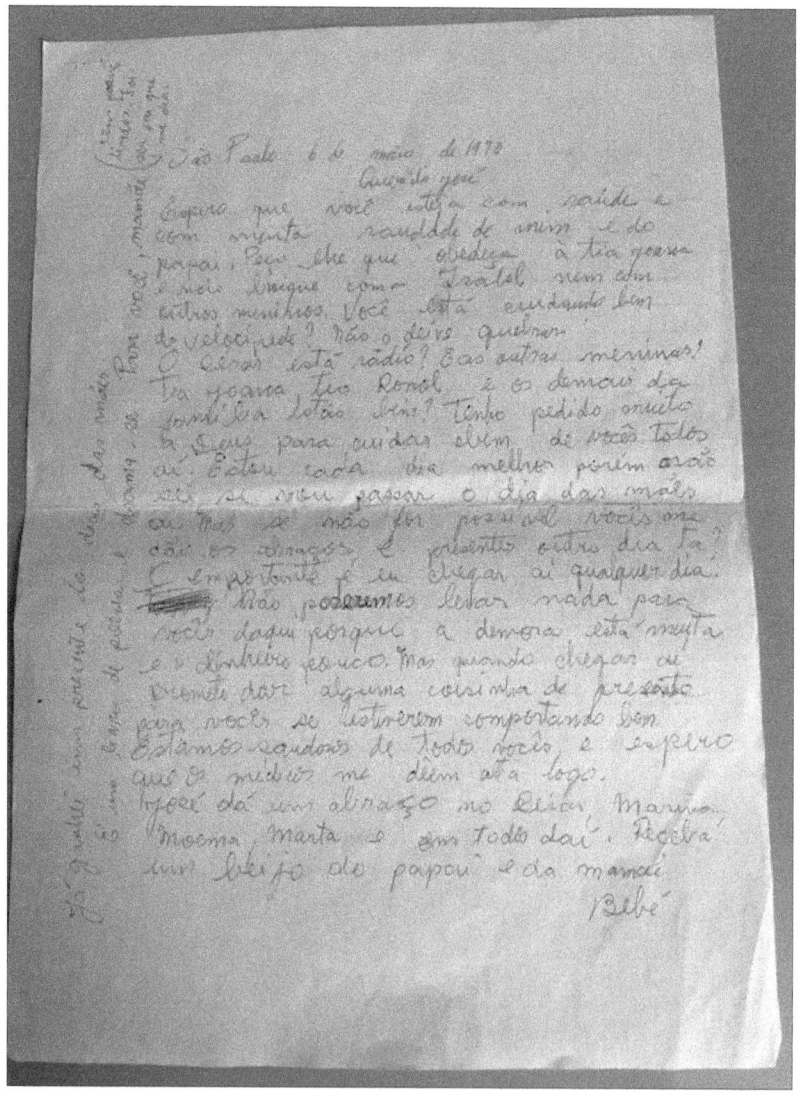

Letter my mother wrote to me in the hospital

I liked cars so much that my father had to buy me a cheap car toy every time I had to get a haircut at his favorite barbershop Antonio's, at the neighborhood market. Antonio was a man who looked like a serial killer with his slick hair with grease and sweat dripping off his face, thick glasses, and a toothpick on the corner of his mouth which he would be chewing on the rhythm of his scissors on my coarse and kinky hair. Every time he used the laser thin serial killer style hand blade to clean my neck and straighten my sideburns and hairline, I thought he was going to murder me and feed my bones to the dozens of stray dogs around his barbershop. That man just scared the bejesus out of me. He would use shaving foam he mixed on this little bowl with warm water, and he would use alcohol to kill the bacteria from the blade, which killed not only the bacteria on his sharp blade but also burnt the skin around my neck and hairline. If my dad got me a cheap metal little car however, I would put up with serial killer Antonio and his barbaric torturing tools and his scary looks, otherwise I would cause havoc and cry and scream and make a scene and most days my father wouldn't have none of it, he'd hold and lift me up by my ears and tell me to shut the fuck up, but occasionally he'd give in. Eventually, being a man of very little patience, he'd get tired of my antics and for the most part I wouldn't get haircuts often enough because they cost my father more than he could afford due to the necessary treat to keep my loudmouth shut. That was the only way I little kid could get something he loved but it didn't always work though.

Wooden toy cars and Lenox

Around and around the sidewalk Isabel Maria pushed me that afternoon and eventually she got tired of it and pushed me inside the house parking me in the living room under this big black four legged with caster wheels table looking thing where we were experiencing an incredibly busy and chaotic foot traffic around it. I recall being so close to the ground inside my wooden fire truck where my cousin had parked me, looking, and trying to guess the owners of the cars parked outside by matching them with the different types of fancy black shining shoes and socks I could see from under this strange table. I couldn't see their faces or bodies and our guests were wearing black clothing, men in suits and women in strange black gowns. I wondered what the occasion was, but I was oblivious to the seriousness of that strange and somber day. Often, I'd rolled myself from under this strange black table to see if I got it right, if the shoes and socks match the cars outside. In one of those peeks to match the shoes, socks and cars, I saw my father with his head on top of the creepy table crying and mumbling some words. I didn't understand what was happening or I didn't want to accept what happened and what brought so many people to our humble home, but these folks were there to pay respect to our family and to my mother who had passed away from Chagas disease at the age of 33 leaving five kids ranging from 1-14 years of age behind and was now in an open casket so friends and family could say their goodbyes.

Chagas (CHAH-gus) disease is an inflammatory, infectious disease caused by the parasite Trypanosoma cruzi, which is found in the feces of the triatomine (reduviid) bug. Chagas disease is common in South America, Central America and Mexico, the primary home of the triatomine bug. Rare cases of Chagas disease have been found in the southern United States, as well.

Also called American trypanosomiasis, Chagas disease can infect anyone. Left untreated, Chagas disease later can cause serious heart and digestive problems.

Treatment of Chagas disease focuses on killing the parasite in acute infection and managing signs and symptoms in later stages.

Triatomine bugs live primarily in mud, thatch or adobe huts in Mexico, South America and Central America. They hide in crevices in the walls or roof during the day, and then come out at night — often feeding on sleeping humans.

Infected bugs defecate after feeding, leaving behind T. cruzi parasites on the skin. The parasites can then enter your body through your eyes, mouth, a cut or scratch, or the wound from the bug's bite.

Scratching or rubbing the bite site helps the parasites enter your body. Once in your body, the parasites multiply and spread.

If Chagas disease progresses to the chronic phase, serious heart or digestive complications may occur. These may include:

- **Heart failure.** Heart failure occurs when your heart becomes so weak or stiff that it can't pump enough blood to meet your body's needs.

- **Enlargement of the esophagus (megaesophagus).** This rare condition is caused by the abnormal widening (dilation) of your esophagus, which can result in difficulty with swallowing and digestion.

- **Enlargement of the colon (megacolon).** Megacolon occurs when your colon becomes abnormally dilated, causing abdominal pain, distention, and severe constipation.

My mother Isabel Gomes Jube lived in thatch and adobe huts when she was a little girl all the way to even after she met and married my father at the age of 16 and carried the disease for many years, untreated. She died of the age of 33 from heart and stomach complications. By her early 20s, she already had a pacemaker put in her heart and she was frail, weak, skinny, and very ill. As a five-year-old boy I didn't understand why my mother was in the hospital when I was telling her about the sound of the cars on the stop light nor do I remember much of my experience with her because she was gone a lot due to the many surgeries and hospital stays in bigger medical centers in Brazil, particularly, Sao Paulo which is about 1000 kilometers from my hometown. My mother got pregnant for the first time when she was 17 years old, and she was told she had a rare disease which made her heart very weak and unable to pump enough blood to the rest of her body. She was told after she gave birth to her first child Marina that she shouldn't get pregnant again and that she was too weak to carry another pregnancy and too sick to take care of kids, her life was already in danger at a very young age. However, she and my father wanted to have a boy and contraceptives were not something that poor people had easy access to back then or even understood enough about it because two years later she had another child, Moema. The doctors were very concerned about mother's health and family and friends helped my father financially to take my mom to Sao Paulo for treatment and better medical care. My parents would go to Sao Paulo and stay for a few weeks at a time while she received specialized care for the rare disease. She would improve from the symptoms and would come back home and be very weak and frail for a while before getting some signs of improvement again. Two years later she would get pregnant again and this time they were for sure expecting a boy but no, my sister Marta was born, and my mother was struggling again and returned to the hospital and treatments ensued, but this time she was getting much weaker and even more frail. A couple of years after she gave birth to Marta, she was forced to get a pacemaker in her heart to assist with the blood pumping deficiency she was suffering from. By this time, she was having other symptoms and her internal organs were failing and causing havoc in her health and in our finances which were non-existent at that juncture.

With unsurmountable odds, an expensive pacemaker, medical and hospital bills, traveling expenses, groceries in Sao Paulo and back home, my parents would never be able to get out of debt and improve not only my mother's health but their quality of life. With no savings or time for work, three very young girls later and not a boy to show for they kept on moving forward and it was a fucking miracle they were still standing.

I guess they didn't think they had enough problems, and she became pregnant again at the age of 28 and was expecting her 4th child after the doctors told her and my father that she shouldn't have more children after the very first, second, and third pregnancies. Ignorance amongst poor, uneducated, and crazy people has a very high price tag eventually. This time she got her first boy, a long and skinny boy whom they named Lenox Gomes Ramos Jube. I was glued to my mother and would be in hospitals and clinics and doctor visits and would be seating next to my mom and use the back of my hand to rub against the cold parts of her upper arms. When one arm got warm, I would move to the other side and rub against the other and so on.

I do not have much memory of my mother however, I remember a couple of things like the rubbing of her arms while seating on an armchair at an aunt's house and a time where my mother washed her hair with egg yolks, honey, and avocado paste in our back yard to soften her curls. Beyond that, it's only what I have been told and things that I read about Isabel Gomes Jube, a daughter amongst eleven siblings herself. She was a teacher in grade school just like one of her sisters Joana. She was tall and lengthy and gorgeous with a hot temper and a knack for teaching according to many stories.

To everyone's surprise, at age 32 she became pregnant once again and this time she gave birth to my brother Cesar who was one year old when she died of heart and stomach complications at the age of 33 on June 2nd, 1970, the same day Brazil played its first-round world cup match against Czechoslovakia (Czech Replublic) and won 4 x 1. I remember watching that match and not really making any sense of such confusing time with euphoric cheers and depressing tears.

The death of my mother was without a doubt the biggest and the most complicated feeling in my life and one I still struggle to manage and understand, although with age I learned to accept it. One of my most difficult challenges was that I didn't have a good size sample of events of my childhood except for the trauma of mother's death and funeral. I see my own kids' uncanny ability to recollect experiences, trips, birthdays, Christmas and life events in general, and for a long time I didn't have any real memory till much later in life thru many hours and resources spent in therapy and working thru the issues which some psychiatrics called Selective Amnesia; a condition, which a child doesn't recollect events after a catastrophe, i.e., the loss of a parent, war, sexual abuse, etc.

After my mother's death I was forever lost in the world and became a child who never felt at peace, never felt loved, never felt cared for even though my sisters did the best they could to take care of me. My sister Marina was only 14 years old when my mother died and she had to cook, clean, go to school, work by making and decorating wooden clothe hangers to sell anywhere people would buy them. We had no mother, and no father who was constantly at work or in bars drinking and looking for ways to get laid…did I mention we had no money either?

I heard so many stories about how my father and his unfaithful ways, about the places where he used to spend his time and the little money he made, while we were at home hungry, desperate, sad, lost and devastated by mother's death. I don't blame my father for anything that happened to us, but I did for a long time resented him for not taking care of my mother with a clearer understanding of what the doctors were trying to tell him. I am not sure if it was my mother's desire to have all these children, or perhaps she was the one who didn't care anymore and kept having babies till her body couldn't take it anymore, but under the many health red flags, it would've been prudent not to take her to the edge of life with one risky pregnancy after another, even if that's what she wanted. The thing is, I never really had the opportunity to talk to my father about that part of his life with my mother. In his midlife, he wasn't someone who would share or dialogue with us kids unless it was one of the great fishing and hunting trips, or the crazy adventures he would embark on with some of my mother's brothers and his adventurous friends.

Perhaps I will never really know why my parents were so ignorant and continued to have children under such harsh conditions who'd have to spend their entire lives searching from the lack of motherly and fatherly love, suffering with depression, sadness, and anxiety not to mention extreme poverty which lasted for a long time till adulthood when we started to lift ourselves from the bottom of the social economic ladder. I don't hold them responsible for many of my tears and all the time, effort, and money I had spent on looking for help, not completely anyways. I have acquired tools and skills to maneuver through life without pointing and blaming others for my misfortunes and found ways to take ownership and agency for my life. I became pretty good at staying open to learning which is forever ongoing but suffering and pain and hardship have always lingered around and been an important part of my journey.

Frustrations and many hours of therapy aside, I am aware that I wouldn't even be here if not for my parents' eagerness to have children even when doctors advised them otherwise. I am forever thankful for the opportunity to have been given the gift of an eventful, rich, challenging, miraculous and beautiful life, which was never promised to be perfect, linear, and always filled with only joy and happiness. Thanks mom and dad, you were crazy and inconsequent young adults but forever my heroes.

CHAPTER II
Cool As The Other Side Of The Pillow

The year my mother died I was sent to school at "Igreja Presbiteriana da Vila Nova." A Cristian church where my mother's sister Joana was a teacher at and my mother's sister-in-law, aunt Nair was the principal. I remember the first day walking with my sister Moema to school and crying all the way from our house to the front gate of the school which was located just about five blocks from where we lived and immediately across from serial killer Antonio's barber shot. What a dichotomy I thought, God and evil just across the street from each other.

The church wasn't all that charming or of any historical significance except that that's where we would go every Sunday except for my father. We participated in Sunday school for a few hours while the adults worshipped inside the main hall. I didn't like going to church at all, I just never felt comfortable there but there wasn't a choice really and church was as part of our Sundays just as the deadly Bayer mosquito spray was part of our nightly routine, suffocating!

Aunt Joana was my mother's older sister and someone who helped my father with his five kids my mother left behind when she died. She and her handsome, blue eyed and blond hair Italian husband Ronol had five children of their own as well and they lived nearby. We could walk to their home from ours and that was just about the best thing in the world for me when I was allowed to go to Auntie Joana's house. She had milk and warm French bread in the morning and always some delicious cake in the afternoons for snack and as a bonus, her husband was nice, kind, soft spoken and a loving father who I wanted to be adopted by. He would call their children by "meu amor" and he had a job as a driver for the city and county that allowed him to have cool cars in his yard and that felt more like my religion and my church to me, cars! Their oldest son Alberto was this tall, skinny blond-haired kid who was charismatic, attentive, and loved cars as well, so I fit right in every time I'd go there, and they seemed to enjoy having me and my sisters around. My sisters and our cousins Marisi, Leila, Helena and Isabel Maria were all about the same age, so they all grew up together and went to the same schools frequented each other's houses all the way to adulthood. We would spend plenty of time with them specially when my father had to leave for a working trip somewhere around the nearby cities. Auntie Joana offered to have some of us kids to live with them because it was too difficult for my father, but he'd have none of that, he'd say, "my kids will be raised by me and that's the end of the discussion." I wouldn't have minded it though; I loved milk and warm bread and the delicious afternoon cake, not to mention uncle Ronol's tenderness towards us. I would take anything over my father's harshness, mate tea every morning and poisonous Bayer spray on a nightly basis…anything!

My first day of school was probably like everyone else's I suppose; a lot of crying, fear, desperation, the butterfly in my stomach and pain in my heart which they never left me to this day every time I see a little kid walking to school or a poor person on the street, just like I would often feel when I went to that school and every new school thereafter. The smells the classroom and later in Sunday school was one of death, mold and old termite infested wood which permeated throughout that place and stayed with me for the longest time.

One of those days while crying and throwing a tantrum at school, which was a constant, I was sent to Auntie Nair principal's office to have me straightened out. She never really asked me why I was crying or consoled this five-year-old who had just lost his mother and was going to school for the first time, she told me to get on my knees next to her desk and she took a ruler from inside her desk drawer and asked me to place the palm of my hands facing up on top of her desk. Not having a clue of what the fuck was about to happen, I obeyed; after all she was the school principal, a godly and devoted christian and my aunt and she must be looking after me, right?

"God doesn't like crying young children, he doesn't like sadness or problems or chaos, the devil does." Spoke aunty Nair with a scary look thru her thick reading glasses which she pushed to the tip of her nose while starring and terrifying the fuck out of me.

I was thinking about evil serial killer Antonio across the street, but I don't recall him talking shit about God or telling me I was a bad boy for crying, telling me to get on my knees, not to be sad or creating havoc to get a haircut. In fact, he never said a word to me, and I cried every time I went to see him and he too had thick reading glasses on the tip of his nose while chewing on that toothpick. He never took out a ruler to beat me up or used his sharp blades to cut me. I was confused between who was God and who was evil.

She then went on to spank the palm of my hands with the ruler dozens of times till the plastic ruler broke in two pieces.

"What the fuck was this woman thinking? Are you serious?" I am wondering while holding my crying inside because I am not allowed to cry I've been told.

She got really mad and went bat shit crazy because she broke her plastic ruler on my hand and was repeatedly murmuring something I couldn't understand. She opened the right top drawer on her wooden desk, took out a longer and thicker wooden ruler this time and resume God's work till I let out a loud cry and asked her to stop because my hands were bleeding already. She didn't stop and she said that God was punishing me for crying every day in school and that I should never forget the lesson I was getting from God thru her and that I should never cry or create problems again otherwise I would be back in her office.

"Please stop, I won't cry or be a problem again, I promise but please stop." I begged without looking at her knowingly full well of my empty promise.

I wish any of those methods of raising and educating a child had worked but they didn't and don't. Those adults screwed us over, they damaged our hearts and our minds, not to mention our emotional intelligence. They physically, mentally and psychologically abused weak and innocent children and showed us some of the worst ways a child should be treated. My aunt Nair, her church goer family and friends and the parenting we experienced with their archaic and violent methods fucked us all up…yes, I point at them for some of the obstacles and my early troubles in life and for most of the later ones too. Motherfuckers!!!

That was the norm, spanked at home, spanked in school, and beaten up on the streets by the bullies around my neighborhood just because I was tall and skinny and had bulgy eyes, bucked teeth and a kinky afro mane style which wouldn't be cut often enough unless I got a stupid toy car. How can a kid grow up and not feel broken and have any reasonable understanding about love and kindness as an adult? I had a lot of work ahead of me for sure.

Auntie Joana never said anything about my hands being all red and bloody from the visit to the principal's office, after all, it was God work and he wanted me to shut the fuck up and stop crying about feeling lonely, desperate, lost, and abandoned by my late mother and my absent father in a new moldy and termite infested church school for five-year-old kids.

I wanted to shout and scream and ask if it was God who was sending all of those nasty kids around my village to beat me up too, but I had no voice, no strength and not an ounce of courage. Fear, desperation, and guilt for being a problem were the only feelings I understood.

She was a religious woman Auntie Joana, and I thought she was nice and would defend me, she went to church couple of times a week besides teaching grade school at the same church/school. She would drag all her kids and all five of us to church on Sundays except for uncle Ronol who would wait outside all morning inside his white DKW Union 1000 S, while smoking a pack of Carlton's.

Carlton cigarettes were not for the average guy but for the well to do ones I figured. They were for people who had a better and higher status in life, folks who drove German cars, drank milk, and had snacks in the afternoon. That's when I started to collect cigarette covers on the streets and playing for them in school where kids would unglue all parts of the cigarette packs, fold them into three sides and use them as if they were dollar bills. I felt rich and had the best collection amongst all the kids in my school and my neighborhood. I had to walk if I wanted to go anywhere and everywhere I walked I would pick up cigarette packs people threw away once they finished smoking the twenty nicotine sticks inside. Nobody really cared to use a garbage can then, just like most humans still don't use them now. I guess things haven't really changed all that much, have they?

Cigarette covers, bolinha de gude (marbles), cheap toy cars, world cup cards, kites and any kind of ball made from old socks stuffed with old newspapers and magazines were my pastime, my refuge, and my salvation.

At school I thought I had family who would show me the ropes and guide me thru a motherless life, but it just didn't feel right, and I didn't want to do that for the rest of my infancy, teenage years, and part of my adult life. School represented a place where I was dropped off, so people wouldn't have to deal with me, that was my thought process. A place where I couldn't cry and have a hard day, or I'd get punished by God and his disciples like Auntie Nair with her fucking wooden rulers. Honestly, life sucked and so did all those beliefs and the people who enforced them upon me.

My sisters were probably very much just as desperate on their own way trying to navigate life without the presence of a nurturing parent, without proper guidance, without feeling love and wanted. How could I expect that they could give me that type of care? But I did, I did expect to have someone to put me on their lap so perhaps I could rub the back of my hands against the cold part of their upper arm and just tell me that things are going to be alright, and we are all going to be just fine. It didn't happen, so I took it to the pillow.

To this day, I flip my pillows pretty much all the time searching for the cool side of it. I don't even think about it, it is just ingrained in my being and something that I've always done. For sure it is a way to continue to search and caress my mother's arms and that soothes me, puts me to sleep and makes me comfortable enough to continue to do life without thinking too much about it, perhaps an unconscious way to cope with what I lacked for so long and a way of not feeling lonely in moments of despair. I am always looking for the cool side of her arms on my pillows.

After a couple of miserable years at Igreja Presbiteriana da Vila Nova school, I was then transferred to Murilo Braga, a public school one block away from my house which I could see from my hideout at the top of the guava tree in my backyard. By seven years of age however, I was already a businessman and a serial entrepreneur in the making. I had thousands of marbles, hundreds and hundreds of rare and fancy cigarettes covers, couple of "futebol" world cup books filled with the best cards and the rarest players, a hand full of kites I had made myself and a few I had acquired by cutting other kid's lines and running after them. I also had a few stuffed balls made with old socks and old newspapers, a few cheap car toys, and a younger baby brother Cesar whom I could play with.

My baby brother Cesar was growing and now I had someone to show all the things I have been learning, someone I could bully around, after all, monkey see monkey do and his existence helped not to feel so lonely all the time. Cesar was this beautiful boy, with bright green eyes, wavy and curly blond hair, a super cute smile, and someone who irked the shit out me from the moment he started to walk. No doubt jealousy and resentment unbeknownst to me was at play. He was clever, loved by all the girls because he was so cute and adorable and had this bubbly personality which I could totally understand why everyone adored and couldn't take their hands off him. He was blessed with good looks, goldilocks curls, gorgeous light and bright green eyes, light skin and a smile that would make everyone melt. He was also talented, he could play soccer at a very young age, and he could play any sport well, even If he never played it before. Naturally talented and gifted he was. He and I would fight all the time and I would ultimately end up being spanked by my father and sisters, mainly Marina who would defend him and still does to this day even if she knew he was wrong. We would play soccer inside the house before my father came home from work which sometimes could be very late. We use my newspaper stuffed in old socks soccer balls with the entrance door as one goal, and the couch legs the other, there were less than 10 feet of space between them on that hallway which was our dream soccer field, and we would lean on the walls and go at each other's throat. We would also dirty the walls and my father would come home from work in a foul mood and get mad, angry, and would make me clean the walls from our dirty hands. This man could see everything and as busy as he was with so much to do and so many kids to tend to, how could he see the stains on the walls?

Cesar and I would pretend we were Vila Nova Futebol Club professional futebol players, my father's favorite soccer club and one he allegedly tried out and played for during his young adult life. We would push and shove and kick each other, and I never let him win but as he got older, I didn't have to, he'd unapologetically whooped me in most of the games we played and would let me know about it…he still does it and we have childish arguments every time we see each other at any family event.

My household was a complete confusion from the perspective of a seven-year-old. I didn't really understand much about my mother being gone and the reasons why she died. I unconsciously erased that event from my memory for a long time till adulthood and pretty much walked around like a zombie much of the time. I wouldn't talk much, didn't like school, didn't have that many friends, didn't have a sibling that was close enough to me both in age and interests due to gender and age differences. My life resumed in waking up, drinking mate tea and having a piece of bread that I picked up from the bakery up the street where I would walk to everyday and get half a dozen mini baguettes which would feed all five of us plus my father. My dad never really ate his in its entirety, he would always leave half of it and the rest of us would fight over the other half like hyenas on a carcass. My older sisters would win often and sometimes they would give it to Cesar because he was still an infant and didn't have any ways to fight for the peace of bread. Tough luck I say!

We would spread margarine on the bread and sprinkle a spoon of sugar on top of it, have a glass of hot mate and everyone would go off to school in the morning except for Marina who would stay home to watch Cesar in the morning and cook our lunch. In the afternoon, she would go to school and my two still teenager sisters would take care of Cesar and make dinner for all of us, usually soup from the scraps from lunch.

Because we only had one bathroom and everyone needed to get ready to go to school, waking up early was a must, otherwise there would be no time to eat before heading out to school on foot. The problem was that my father also would wake up early and he would take forever in the bathroom without any regard for time and our needs to use the facility. He would take a shower every morning and his showers were so long that sometimes we had to go on the yard to do our business because he just took his sweet old time and didn't care. We couldn't say anything, we couldn't knock on the door or ask him to hurry up, there wasn't any sympathy for us kids and to talk about it was completely out of our realm of possibilities. We had to accept that he was the king, and you just don't fucking question the king. Every time he got out of the shower, we could see all the steam coming from his still wet body with the bathroom walls and the small vanity mirror all fogged up and wet, ramping up the discomfort and already hot and humid small house. We would rush in there and sometimes there would be two or three of us at the same time, brushing teeth, using the toilet, or taking a shower. The toilet bowl would be completely wet with his foot marks on it and from the splashing water because there was no shower curtain or shower doors and since there was no toilet seat cover, we either had to seat on it wet or dry it with our hands if we wanted to use it. Toilet paper was rationed in our house and in Brazil we don't throw toilet paper in the toilet bowl, we couldn't waste any toilet paper on drying the edges of the toilet bowl because there were too many of us and not enough toilet paper to go around. My father would walk out of the shower and go into his bedroom, put a shirt on and get the Johnson Oil bottle and spread it on his wavy hair. He would then get his Flamengo plastic comb and fix his hair front to back, put some alcohol on his face because he would shave after showering and I could hear him tapping on his neck and face because the alcohol would burn his skin and he would cuss things like:

"Oh desgraça, filho da puta," "fuck, son of a bitch," as he would tight his belt around his jeans, take half of his mini baguette and walk out the door. He never offered to take us to school…ever!!! I was never dropped off at school by my father or anybody else except for that first day when I was five years old when Moema walked me to school, but nobody else had that privilege either. His car was for his use and his work and whatever we needed we had to get it ourselves otherwise it wasn't going to happen. My sisters Moema and Tata went to the same school at Instituto de Educacao de Goiania – IEG. They had to wear school uniforms that consisted of blue skirts and white shirts which had to be hand washed, hung on the clothing wire outside, dried and pressed every single day, rain or shine. They only had one skirt and one white shirt each and were not allowed to attend classes without uniforms. We all walked to school, no matter how close or how far it was, there was no money to catch a bus and no rides from anyone albeit my father or friends and family, we had to walk fast and make sure we weren't late, or we would get spanked for getting tardy warnings on our grade reports.

My father had some type of temper, he not only would beat my mother and have horrific fights with her, but he would come home a little tipsy at times and if things weren't how he expected in the house, which they never were because his expectations were completely unrealistic, he would scream and shout and call my sisters names and sometimes- more often than not- beat them up too. He would spank them for just about anything, there was never a conversation about any subject when he was home, it was usually just tension and fear of him needing something and us unable to provide it to the king in a timely fashion. If he needed to fix a door jam or a leaking faucet, he would scream to one of us to bring him his tools and if we didn't find it quickly (we never did), he would get really mad, frustrated and impatient and whoever was given the task to get him his screw driver or some bolts, he would call us names, he would curse and sometimes even beat us up to teach us a lesson and make sure we'd never move his tools from where he thought they were… thing is, the tools were never there where he'd tell us or maybe the stress and pressure to have to find it and find it quickly would get to us and it was just pure hell if he ever needed to fix anything in our house which everything was always broken, from our hearts and souls to our faucets and doors, everything was broken. Those days felt like so long, and I don't know how we didn't kill each other or got killed by my father in the process. We would get yelled at for absolutely nothing and spanked for much less.

As crazy as this might sound, I wasn't spanked as much as my sisters were, however. The violence towards them got to a point that he would hit them with the clothes iron electric cord and their legs would be completely marked, sometimes cut, bruised and bleeding. They would be embarrassed to put their skirts on and go to school but there was no choice and no hiding, this is what he knew, this is how he learned from a very young age, this is how he was raised and how he was treated by his parents and his older brother. This was how his friends treated their kids and their spouses as well. How can you expect anyone to practice kindness, nurturing, love, and affection when you never received any of it yourself? When you don't even know what it means to be patient, to have a dialogue, an understanding that we were just kids trying to survive in a world without a mother and without a loving father, what the fuck? Why couldn't the guy just for once ask us a simple question about how we were feeling? How was school? I never heard a single "I love you" from my father till the later years of his life but by then I had already done too many of "I love yous" in front of a mirror or in a couch at a therapist's office and I was already fucked.

One would think that these types of behaviors only happened in the movies or in other people's lives. I sometimes would get paralyzed with the shouting and the screaming of my father and my sisters, the lack of consideration and love for us young boys who were watching this and learning by proxy, that this is how we treat women, how we treat kids, how we treat human beings. I don't think I have even seen that much abuse and hatred anywhere else before and have never seen it after I left home in the many other households I frequented and families I met along the way…never and nothing even close to what we endured.

Not surprising to me, that type of constant abuse taught me how to be selfish, egocentric, narcissist, and manipulative. It thought me that in order to survive, I needed to find a way out of there before I also turned into a violent man, one with addictions, emotionally broken, ignorant, impatient, and filled with rage. I had to get out of there so I wouldn't hit my kids the same way in the future. In fact, I didn't want to have any kids ever, I didn't think it was fair or right to put children in this world and not shower them with love and affection, and I was afraid that I may not have either one of those traits in me.

CHAPTER III

The Green Lizard

In January of 1973, last than three years after my mother's death, my father remarried, this time the victim was Leonidia Maria Lacerda Ramos Jube, his second and distant cousin and someone 11 years his junior. I'd never met Nida (that was her nickname) before except for a brief encounter while traveling thru the old capital of Goias Velho where we would go for weekends occasionally and where my father and Nida were born. Goias Velho is an old historic town which used to hold the title of State Capital of Goias. The city is mostly paved with huge uneven boulders and cobble stones and the homes are mostly butting against one another with people sharing the same side walls. If anyone had a yard, it could only be in the back because no front yard or any side separation from neighbors existed. The walls must have been built of a very good insulating mud because you couldn't hear anything coming from the neighbors. Most people spent their time people watching from their old and colorful double-hung sash wooden windows, gossiping, and hearing the rice cake man sell their delicious rice cakes on the streets and screaming; "Olha o bolo de arroz" (check out the rice cake). They were warm, fluffy muffin like homemade cakes sold everywhere around town and a tradition which is still alive in Goias Velho to this day.

Nida was a shy, beautiful 30-year-old distant second cousin of my father's who's never been married although she had been engaged to a gentleman in Itapirapua, a small little town 170 kilometers from Goias Velho where she'd been teaching literature and writing at a middle school.

A few months after we went on that trip to Goias Velho to meet Nida, my father asked her to marry him, which to this day I still wonder how desperate and innocent a woman must had been to marry a man with five young children ranging from 3 to 16 years of age, financially broke and a complete mess of a human being. That's how I perceived my father and our family, a mess, a train wreck.

Sure, my father was a handsome and charming fella when he wanted to be but with all that baggage and a truckload of small children, it had disaster written all over it. From a child's perspective who didn't have much experience with the feelings of nurturing and love, I never understood Nida's motivation but perhaps she saw in us kids a need for a mother and she wanted to help us...Maybe she thought she was getting old and wanted to get married and raise a family of her own and make her family proud, truth is I don't know, and it doesn't really matter. Many years later when she was going thru the same things my mom went thru, I asked her why she married my dad with all those red flags, and she told me while crying:

"I love him." Nida replied while sobbing and crying which she rarely did.

Go figure, love is the damnedest thing!

In later years with noticeable deteriorating health and visible sadness, I encouraged her to leave my father a few times but to no avail, she indeed loved him or perhaps was too afraid or too embarrassed to be divorced...she never left. I loved Nida though, she was an angel who came down from heaven to watch over and protect us. For sure she went thru a lot of rejection and rebellion from all five of us and specially my sisters who were not happy with having a stepmother just couple of years after my mom died. Nida was one of the most beautiful and patient human beings I have ever met in my life, she taught us so much and she protected us from my father as much as she could, but she never suffocated or stopped us from exploring life and nurturing our curiosity. There were times when there was nothing she could do though; she would beg him not to hit us, but he would ignore her and if she got on his way, she'd get it too...and she did.

I know that for many years she felt powerless, ignored, neglected, cheated, disrespected, beaten, used, and abused. She never told me these things, or shared it with anyone else for that matter but she didn't need to, in fact she never really complained about anything, and I'd always admired her so much for her pure heart and quiet strength. I felt her pain, we all felt her pain and always tried to protect her in return, but we were unbale at times just like she was unable to protect us in others. She would fight in her own quiet ways, sometimes she simply lowered her head, took the abuse, and moved on with hopes for better days, I guess. Nothing else could explain to me what she was doing there under such extenuating circumstances when she had so much ahead of her, she was such a beautiful woman and an exceptional human being besides being well educated and very intelligent...well, one might argue that given her choice for a husband, perhaps she was in cahoots with my late mother to get some revenge of sorts.

Nida came into our lives to teach us courage, patience, and love and she did much more than that, she inspired us all when she went back to school at age fifty while pregnant of Saulo, her third and my father's eighth child. She wanted a higher degree which would contribute to our finances bottom-line, and she did that too. We were all in awe of her strength, her resolve and shear courage to spend another two years in a classroom while raising seven kids and pregnant of another, cook, wash, clean, and on top of all of that: be a wife of a brute and abusive man without ever losing her fucking marbles. I am exhausted just writing about it and this saint of a woman stayed for almost 30 years and all she did was teach us to be better humans without ever even trying, because that's who she was, an awesome human...I miss her. We were ever so lucky, and she was always such a role model, the one we were craving for.

At the Nossa Senhora da Aparecida church na cidade de Areias, Jose Simao Ramos Jube and Leonidia Maria Lacerda Ramos Jube exchanged vows and got married in front of about forty people and a huge green lizard. The church was and still is this small old white and blue chapel on top of the hill built in 1780 with 87 steps of concrete stairs surrounded by big cactus leaves where visitors would write their names, messages, their promises, and prayers on them, as if the plants were their way thru God, and there those messages stayed for dozens of years if not longer till the cactus leaves grew old and died. That church has a big significance in our lives because that's where my father was baptized, where he would go with his grandfather who supposedly owned a huge piece of land right across the highway which can be seen from the church courtyard on the hillside. The land was so vast that my dad used to say that "everything you see around here, from this gate to the top of those mountains and as far as your eyes can reach, it all belonged to my grandfather." But somehow, which was never explained to us, got all taken away from the family and there was nothing left except misery and poverty.

"Fuck, can we ever get a break?" I would often murmur to myself when I heard that story.

The wedding ceremony was beautiful, short and sweet. Nida was dressed in a white, simple, humble but tasteful wedding gown and my father was sporting a linen grey suit which I assumed someone made for him as a gift because he had absolutely no money to pay for a beautiful linen suit like that. Nida was like always, an angel, in fact I think she should've had wings on her wedding dress because I was convinced, she was an angel without a shadow of doubt. My father looked the part; he was his charming self, with his deep blue eyes, a black mustache that would make Tom Selek envious. His wavy hair was well groomed and oiled, his skin was glowing, and he was happy, he seemed very happy and proud to have found such a great catch in Nida: A teacher, eleven years younger, no children, no previous marriages, no baggage, in fact I wouldn't be surprised if Nida was still a virgin at the age of 30 when she married my father.

In the middle of that small church and all the gorgeous vintage wooden benches and furniture, there was a small rock altar which was made by the slaves who built that church by hand, one big boulder at a time in the late 1700's for their owners and their families to worship on Sundays. Behind the rocky altar was a tall and elegant Catholic Priest who was conducting the wedding ceremony. When he turned to Nida and asked her if she would take my father as her husband, honor him, respect him, cherish and be loyal to him, a huge green lizard jumped from the ceiling to the rock alter and landed on top of the Priest's bible. Everyone got spooked when Nida let out loud scream, confused, as the priest took a step backwards while watching the green reptile on top of his "Livro Sagrado." The Lizard just stayed there on top of the bible moving its head from left to right as if it was trying to say something…

"Get the fuck out of there Nida!" That would be my guess. There was this split moment of disbelief and surprise with some people giggling at the bizarre scene. The elegant priest chuckled, shrugged his shoulders and looked at Nida waiting for her response.

"Yes I do." Replied Nida.

Noooooo, I thought. I truly believe that the lizard was my mother trying to tell Nida to get the fuck out of dodge, to run for her life and never look back while she still could. My father put a ring on her finger and our lives were forever changed, again…for the most part, for better.

CHAPTER IV
The Sacrificial Bird

O n Sundays, we watched every Formula 1 race on TV as a family. My dad would do the cooking with Nida that day, usually there would be some friends over or some family members who stopped by to visit and get a bite of the awesome food. The dichotomy of our household was that people loved to come by and pay a visit. Friends and our extended family members enjoyed being around my father, and that to us was something we never really understood. Especially on Sundays, folks would flock over to partake on the awesome Sunday lunches and my father treated them exactly the way we could only dream on being treated: with respect, kindness, attention, with funny jokes and with love. We would seat in front of our boxy three channel Philips TV and watch the pre-race show all morning before we go out to play until he called us for lunch. Sundays were his favorite; he would be a little more loose and friendly and he loved to cook the Sunday meals. Early Sundays he'd venture into the village farmer's market a few blocks from our house and buy fresh corn, okra, a truly free-range and alive chicken, rice, potatoes, and red beans. He would come home with the bird upside down hanging on one of his arms and flapping its wings and making all kinds of noises, that poor bird knew what was about to go down and it was trying to escape at any cost from the moment it saw my father coming.

My father would bring all the stuff inside this old and rusty broken-down grocery cart he put together with some scraps from the backyard. The first thing he would do was cut that chicken loose in the backyard and let it roam around before the sacrificial ceremony took place. In the meantime, he prepped the mash potatoes, unhusk the corn cobs and scraped them with an old fishing knife which was methodically sharpened on a limestone rock in the backyard under a stubby water spigot as he ran water on the blade and pressed it against the stone while flipping that knife from one side to the other. He'd scrape the corn from the cob into a big bowl, minced couple of whole onions enough to make everyone near the kitchen get teary eyes, he'd smash the garlic and mixed with the onions, salt, a bit of beer, spices and vinegar into an old iron cast garlic smasher. With a wooden stick he would mix everything and make a paste, which we could smell the spicy and familiar aroma of garlic, onions, and chives concoction from a block away from the house. It is an aroma that stayed with me to this very day, and on every occasion I cook, I often do it with fresh garlic and onions, I can feel my father's spirit, I can sense his presence and hear his heavy steps moving around the kitchen with such delicate precision and care. Thru food we connected in meaningful ways, thru colors and textures we found our common ground, thru the sweet aroma of fresh garlic and onions and the delicious dishes my old man put together, we coexisted and let love be bigger than hatred and resentment. My father left plenty of scars but also those sweet aromas ingrained in all of us as if he was trying to say "I love you" to our face but the only form of communication he knew was thru his impeccable attention to details in the kitchen and his beyond delicious food. We could see it clearly in our Sunday dishes how much love this complicated and difficult man put into those Sunday meals. We knew it was all for us because he was never a big eater. I've always felt he wanted to express his sorrow, his regret and his happiness thru food, and he did more than that!

On Sunday we could play outside before lunch as long as we didn't break any light bulbs or crack any windows which would completely change the mood around the house. He'd go ballistic and ape shit nuts with the ball hitting one of his light bulbs in the garage or the front glass door in front of the house which had to be replaced couple of times due to an inadvertent soccer ball finding its way into our front porch glass door. Right in front of our corner house there was a light post and a big enough of a tree to be another post for the soccer goal that would become the training ground of many aspiring goal keepers, midfielders, and forwards around the neighborhood. In one of the higher branches, there was an old and rusted aluminum garbage can, nailed to a high enough crouch of the tree. There, many of the fellas in the neighborhood would emulate the likes of Oscar Robertson, and later Larry Bird and Magic Johnson and would meet and play there and dream about these incredible superheroes of mine. We all talked smack and pick on each other but often succumbed to the reality that it was fucking impossible for us to ever achieve that kind of stardom, or that we would ever have a chance to see or meet one of those guys in our in real life one day. We could talk about what we would say to them if we were playing against them or were teammates one day. I would talk trash to them and pretend I was dunking on Magic's face after a pass from Bird.

"Take that Magic, get up cus there's more coming your way, get up boy!" I'd scream at Magic Johnson loudly and obnoxiously and everyone would laugh at me and probably wonder "what the fuck was I mumbling about?"

The main players in our soccer team were: Myself, Cesar, our cousin Adriano, and neighbors Pedrinho, Renatinho, Pudim (all brothers), Ze Preto, Gordo who were raised by this woman named Ana Maria who had adopted them both from different orphanages. Luizinho, the best player of all of us, and Hernani who own the Adidas Samba soccer ball and the yellow and black uniforms which would be all clean and neatly folded before each match. Hernani was also the goalkeeper when Gordo couldn't play or was having a brain freeze moment, which he often would go thru during a match. Sometimes he looked better than Gigi Buffon (best Italian goalkeeper ever) and other times he was as bad as Valdir Perez (worst Brazilian goalkeeper ever). So, when the spirit of Valdir Perez possessed Gordo, we'd sacked him, insert Hernani in and give Gordo a break for him to gather his thoughts and snap the fuck out of it.

Hernani was the only kid in our neighborhood who had any money. He had expensive goalie gloves, long sleeve padded jerseys, elbow pads, knee pads and great goalie cleats with padded high socks. He couldn't play for shit but he looked damn good and he owned the Adidas ball and the unis. His father was some big shot figure in the courts in downtown and they had a very nice VW Brazilia which I was totally jealous of. They lived in a house with expensive gates which we couldn't see anything from the outside, but we knew there was a swimming pool, a bbq area and even a coveted ping pong table, rich people for sure and we were never really invited there, we weren't classy or clean enough to come inside Hernani's home.

We would give names to some of the games we invented on Rua 217 #11 corner with Rua 200. "Cu de Boy," "Golzinho," "Golzao." There were too many ways to play soccer that I have never seen being played since. I don't think we saw anybody doing what we were doing, and honestly I don't know how we came up with those games because we didn't really watch TV and saw it been played, except for the big soccer matches or the World Cup every four years. We were pioneers of so many ways to play soccer, sometimes even without a real ball, without goals or enough players.

The basketball games were different though, not everyone enjoyed playing it or knew how except for me and Adriano Andrade, my rich cousin, with great hair, and a sweet VW bug on cream color to his name were the ones who had epic battles on that street court.

My father would come out in between the Sunday dish prep sometimes holding a small glass with some cold Antartica Beer in one hand and the bottle for refilling it on the other. He would seat on the porch and watch and laugh at our silly games. Those moments were the only time my dad ever watched me play any sports up to that point in my life. Being a former soccer player that he was, he probably thought we were a bunch of idiots and morons, eventually he would say; "Ok everybody, inside… let's go get that chicken now." He would never have to say things twice, when my father would give us an order, everyone understood that he meant fucking now!!! When our friends and neighbors heard my father giving us an order, they'd split as fast as they could and ran home. They were scared shitless of my old man, and so were we, but we didn't have a place to run to. Everyone in that neighborhood heard my old man scream and yell at us from their homes often and I can only imagine the rumors and what they thought of our family. I am sure they were too afraid to say anything or even ask what all the shouting and crying was all about. Discrete fellas I'd say!

Now inside the house and following my father's orders, we pass by the TV in the living room and they would still be showing interviews and the life style of the rich and famous Formula 1 racers and their gorgeous women, their helicopter commute to work or their private jets, their gigantic and fancy homes, their motorhomes and yachts and how cool they were…I was like; "yeah, that's what I want for me, but I am too fucking tall to fit in those tiny race cars though…shit I can never get a break!" I'd say often.

We would go to the backyard and my dad would explain to us that the reason he'd bring the chicken home alive from the market was because he wanted it to be stressed and hot blooded, tense, and scared like a motherfucker before he'd kill it and cook it.

"This fucking bird doesn't need to be more scared man, just by being singled out by those deep blue eyes amongst a bunch of other birds at the market should be traumatic enough." That was my thinking.

My father had first-hand knowledge from his childhood experiences of stealing chickens and pigs that it tasted better when they were stressed, hot blooded, rushed, and scared, that it would make its meat more tender and tastier. How can one argue with that type of empirical knowledge? That Sunday lunch was the best meal I have ever had in my life. It was exact the same for many years, more than 40 years till Nida died, and it always tasted incredibly amazing and out of this world soulful, and religiously loved by everyone that were ever lucky enough to try it.

We'd run after that chicken till we completely tired the motherfucker out, and it tired us just as badly. It would be cornered a few times and would find its way thru under our legs or over our heads and it would flap and kick, poop, and scream and perform just about all kinds of moves and escape tricks that UFC fighters would love to add to their repertoire. However, It would always escape us till my dad show up, very calmly, ask us to be quiet and that poor bird knew that its days were over, it was about to have his neck twisted and hang upside down and there was nothing it could do about it. My father would throw some dried corn flakes on the dirt and the moment that bird went for the treats, with one swift move my father would grab it by its neck and perform a 360 degree spin and twist, break its neck, tie his feet again and hang it up side down on a broken branch off our guava tree. While hanging upside down, the little fella would enter a comatose state, convulsion and slow death. This chicken would try to move its broken neck and flap its wings but "no can do;" snapped neck, spine completely fucked-up and all its blood now rushing to the head in a dramatic finale while having its last attempt of survival. It was taking its final breath and it had to succumb to being appreciated as a consolation prize soon to be in our plates in pieces, swimming in a sauce with fresh corn and okra, and the best mash potato a human can ever taste.

From the guava tree branch it would go to the boiling water where it would be "depenado" (plucked). My father had already a huge pot with boiling water going on in our backyard near the mango tree. He had prepared it in advance and now it was time to sink that bird in boiling water after all the torture and the suffering from all that running and escaping a bunch of crazy kids and the broken neck business. Once sunken into boiling water for a few minutes, the feathers would all come out very easily and in a matter of minutes the whole bird was dead, featherless, and completely bald and cleaned.

But wait a minute! If that type of torture wasn't enough, and to make matters worse for that two-legged bug eating creature, it was now time to burn its feet. Yes, my father would hold the bird to the fire by removing the boiling pot from the fire pit he'd set up with old charcoal he'd made from the backyard pieces of wood laying around and burn its tights and feet all the way around to "sapecar" and remove all the tough feather stubbles, which wouldn't come out with the boiling water.

This whole process from twisting its neck and watching the thing die, took about 5 minutes as some were more defiant than others and would fight for longer but none of those once free range, roaming around corn flake bug eaters ever survived, and they all ultimately ended up making our Sunday meals the best and happiest times of our lives and one of the few moments which I'd always looked forward to in our house…besides running away!

How can this poor bird not taste exceptionally good? This son of a bitch went from roaming freely in somebody's backyard, eating whatever he wanted and doing whatever it pleased, to being chased after by a bunch of lunatic and hungry kids, tortured with a broken neck by a scary blue eyed crazy man, hung upside down till it succumbed to its death, sunk in boiling water, its feet and legs burnt and then chopped into small pieces, fried and slowed cooked to perfection to feed a bunch of scared, confused and always very hungry people…sounds like perfection to me!

Each one of us had a favorite piece which was well documented and not open for discussion, ever. My father loved the neck which was always filled with small bones and all the blood from the hanging upside down before the bird's death. Nida enjoyed eating and sucking on the head's tiny bones, not much meat there but she'd spend her sweet time patiently going thru every little piece of dark meet in her plate which she always ate with her hand while seating on the stairway leading to our kitchen. Marina was into the liver and its neck which she and Nida would share it often. Moema loved the gizzard, and she too would take her time to clean every small and big bone which still had any meat on it. Tata was into the coveted soft and juice butt which she would fight with everyone about it and always win. Cesar liked the big tights; he would always argue with those who didn't think it was fair that he got to eat both of them but at times my dad made him share with Sergio because the tights were too big for a small kid like that. Sergio was crazy about the dark pieces and one of the tights he was sometimes allowed to have but he'd also be awarded the wings and back which had very little meat for the bird was deep fried first before being slow cooked in a beautiful broth with all the other veggies and his favorite back bones, which would completely melt in his mouth. Sandro was into the lower chest and the white and chunky single piece Nida would garnish his plate with such delicate and loving touch; rice on the bottom, one big spoon of beans evenly spread over the rice and then the big prize of white meat on top of it all finishing the garnishing with as much sauce, corn and okra it could fit in those white and chipped on the borders small and deep aluminum old plates in our house. Saulo loved the tasty sauce with the corn, okra and all the aromatic spices too but he just ate whatever Nida put in his plate, he was too small to choose or fight about anything. As for me, I loved the upper breast, but it wasn't so much for the taste which was always phenomenal but rather for the "Y" looking bone that held the breast together and after I devoured that succulent and heavenly tasty piece of happiness, my father would play a game with me. He would tell me to hold on to one side of the Y bone and he'd hold onto the other end, he'd count one, two, three and we both pull causing it to break into two, whomever ended up with the bigger side of the Y, win the game. The game in my head was always to get the bigger piece and if I succeeded, I'd win an imaginary pick-up truck and a place of my own and a telephone one day. I'd win often and my entire life and happiness hinged on that bone and the manifestation of my dreams attached to it.

What I missed the most however was seating on that crooked and broken dining table with the flannel print tablecloth, all the plates and silverware set in perfectly order, and everyone around anxious to dig into the best meal of our lives and see all those beautiful dishes our parents spent all day preparing for us. Did I mention the spectacular mash potato?

It was happy times on Sunday afternoons, everyone seemed happy and well fed. My father was usually nice, soft and his love and care for his family was evident from the time he woke up to get to the farmers market till the moment we all finished every single dish accompanying that kitchen casserole, washed, cleaned the entire kitchen, and put all the dishes away in a cramped roach infested blue aluminum cabinet.

Besides chicken, the menu consisted of rice, beans, mash potatoes, lettuce, cucumber and tomato salad and every now and then there would be a bonus; the infamous spaghetti Bolognese with olives, sliced hard boiled eggs and shredded parmesan cheese on top, which we all waited to eat at the end of our meal as if it was a special prize, a gift from the heavens above which we would mix the spaghetti with the beans and the spicy sauce swimming in our plates…If I could replicate that taste, texture and feeling, I would but it's one of those time stopping moments of my life which will live only in my memories…and my siblings all feel the same way.

CHAPTER V
Eaten by the Jungle?

B y September of 1973, our clan had grown to six kids with another baby boy on his way. After the wedding Nida was immediately pregnant of Sergio and less than a year after, she was giving birth again of her second child, Sandro. There was a pattern here and one which didn't end well last time with my mother and the consecutive pregnancies.

The Jube family now consisted of my father, Nida, Marina, Moema, Marta, Lenox, Cesar, Sergio, about to be born Sandro and Zippy, our chihuahua pooch. Life was still however unexplainably chaotic and tense, lacking just about everything, and not much fun. My family was a mess, the household was stressful and too complicated for a kid to understand and much less be able to dream about anything...but yet, I dreamt. I dreamt about growing up and being out of the toxic environment I was being raised in. I dreamt about having dreams, aspirations, and desires and worked constantly on not being fearful of the future and how to leave that life for good. I dreamt big and I dreamt about that sexy motorcycle that would take me to beautiful and twisty roads one day without any rear mirrors. I dreamt about leaning on the corners imagining each turn as the wind would blow onto my face and blow my hair back like I used to see in the James Bond movies.

I dreamt of riding thru plenty of mud and gravel so I could enjoy the sliding of the tires under me and feel the butterflies in my stomach, the uncontrollable palpitations of my heart as I'd come close to falling off the motorcycle, but I'd always save it. I would lay down on my bunk bed and

41

stare at that moldy ceiling for hours, in a constant voyage to nowhere, but anywhere out of that house. I was tired of the fights and the constant tension, the lack of food, the violence, the yelling and screaming in the middle of so many sleepless nights, tired of the emotional, mental and physical abuse we were all living under. I dreamt of somewhere where I wouldn't have to be afraid of every move I make and every step I'd take because that's how it was at home, a constant state of fear and guilt and I didn't know how to behave inside or outside of the house.

We'd tried our best to be in bed by the time the king would come home but the arguments would ensue the moment he'd walk thru the door, and it was always about where he'd been all night. I remembered more than a few times when the kitchen table and chairs were flying and thrown around, putting holes on the walls with the loud and nasty fights which would end up in physical and not to mention plenty of verbal abuse. My mother went thru and now I witnessed Nida going thru it in a way that it would break my heart but there was nothing a kid could do except to freeze and numb his feelings and pretend that nothing was happening. I'd cover my ears and numb myself by staring at my blank canvas above my bunkbed and dreamt about dreaming freely one day, far away from that nightmarish of a life while manifesting an eventual escape.

Often, I would hear their arguments when Nida would ask my father about the cheap cologne or the lip stick on his shirt collar. I wanted to be a hero so many times and confront him and tell him that what he was doing was wrong, that he was not only hurting Nida the same way he hurt my mother but also, he was showing us kids all the wrong examples of how not to be a good man, a good human, a good husband, and a descent father. I had those thoughts as far back as five years old.

One of those many late nights he came home tipsy and angry at the world, he told us that we would be moving to Porto Velho, a small town in the middle of the Amazon Forest in the northwest part of the country. I'd heard of the Amazon before and how huge and important to the planet it was but moving there was not any part of my daily dreams when staring at my ceiling above my bunkbed...no sir!

"What the fuck, are you kidding?" I was rapid firing the whole experience in my confused mind.

The other aspect of the trip which he waited to tell us till the end of his announcement was how we were going to get there…by car.

"It will be a beautiful three to four-day driving experience thru the Amazon Forest, it will be great." Said my father with no expression on his face, dismissive of the obstacles ahead.

A three-day trip of 3,500 kilometers from our town of Goiania to Porto Velho thru dirt roads on the Amazon Forest, which it seemed doable except two thirds of the way were of dirt and muddy Transamasonica Highway which was just in the early stages of being deforested let alone paved. The other caveat was the amount of people who would be making this journey inside a black 1969 three-cylinder two door Ford Corcel, license plate Goiania, AC 2929. The car was bought from one of my uncles and it was in great shape mainly because my father always took better care of his cars than he did of his children and wives. He would wash it every Sunday, make us help him polish it and wash the wheels while he checked on oil and fluids and tire pressure. Till the day he died, he took great care of the vehicles he owned. In fact, I bought from his estate the last truck he owned and one which I bought for him in one of my trips to Brazil in mid 2000's. A 2006 Chevy S10 which my brother Cesar keeps and takes care of it in Rio de Janeiro. The truck was and still is in great shape and I hope to keep it till the day I die.

The trip to Porto Velho was going to take about three to four days as my father sold it to us and the five kids plus my father and pregnant Nida and our little pup Zippy were all going to fit into the two door Ford Corcel. My oldest sister Marina who had started university was going to stay back and live with our aunt Cro, her husband Sebastiao and our cousin Mirian who was and still is close to Marina and about the same age.

We didn't know any better so the thought of five kids, my father, a pregnant woman, and a dog, inside of a small two door compact car didn't faze us…nothing did. Our luggage and food supplies were supposed to last the three to four days thru the fucking Amazon Forest and it seemed just like what the doctor ordered, NOT!!!

Truth is we had done many trips cramped inside a compact two door car before but never for that long. However, one of the qualities my father had was that he was a great driver, and he could make it interesting with so many stories to share during our journey. For better or for worse, we saw the trip to the Amazon as a much-needed change, new environment, new friends, new school, new home, and the prospect of my father and all of us making a better living.

"This will be an unforgettable trip; it will be great, and I will have my own business too. C'mon cheer up." Said my father in a tone of voice we have never heard before.

He was excited and hopeful now, and I didn't sense the fearfulness so often camouflaged in tyranny.

The first part of our trip turned out to be plenty of fun, my father was in a good mood, he too was dreaming for better days and excited for the opportunity to be a partner at a new mechanic shop in the middle of the Amazon. It was very promising due to the many companies and people in their trucks and buses venturing into the Northeast part of the country in search of a better life.

When we got to Cuiaba, in Mato Grosso, after 900 kilometers of paved asphalt into our journey we encountered our first real challenge and one I will never forget. The weather had been very wet which is very typical in that part of the country, and we had been traveling under constant rainstorms in the last 400 or so kilometers. When we got to this small bridge, we noticed there was a line of cars and trucks waiting to cross it. My father told us to stay inside the car and said he was going to check things out.

Curious that I am, I stepped out of the car despite everyone's protest to see what was going on. I could see how the creek had turned into a small river overflowing the bridge with a strong current capable of washing away cars, trucks and people adventurous enough to try the crossing to the other side.

I noticed from afar my father on top of the bridge railing with water just about couple of inches from his feet talking to some folks and checking the depth and the current strength. The rain got heavy again as my father got back and told us that we all needed to step out of the car, take all our luggage and belongings and take the pedestrian walkway which was a small bridge a few feet higher than the one he was about to attempt the suicide mission of crossing with our Ford Corcel.

"I will be crossing by myself, meet me on the other side." Said the king confidently.

As always, we didn't think it was a good idea, but we weren't dumb enough to challenge my father on anything, especially when it came to cars and driving. He was astute, a risk taker and someone with a lot of experience and confidence, and anything related to cars, trucks, bridges, and machines, he was an expert and to be honest, it was fun to watch him in action and learn or just be a mere observant of his prowess. He also had a stint at DERGO (Department of Roads of Goias) for a few years building roads, fixing their machines, and building bridges, he had experience with the task at hand for sure, but this flooded bridge crossing was sketchy.

He revved up the 3-cylinder Ford Corcel engine and charged onto the water overflowing the bridge. The car danced from one side of the completely flooded bridge onto the other and we could see the smoke coming from under the hood and water flooding the car all the way to my father's chest. I have no idea how he figured in his mind; "yes, I can drive thru this and get to the other side, no problem."

"Really? Are you fucking serious man?" I was convinced once and for all that it wasn't that my father was crazy, no…he simply had a complete different set of skills and beliefs, he was completely fearless as if he was always defying logic or perhaps his logic and fear levels were above most mere mortals. It seemed he lacked any common sense, but he knew what he was doing. He kept the car going alright, and made it to the other side but, deep inside of me there was some small hope that the river could do us a huge favor and take everything at once, including my father and his beloved Ford Corcel. What we didn't account for was Zippy, our little spotted black and white chihuahua, we forgot him inside the car, and he was swimming from front to back, left to right inside the flooded car. I could see his little scary eyeballs bulging thru the back window staring at us as he probably thought this whole trip was dog shit crazy.

My father not only made it thru the flooded bridge on his three cylinders Ford Corcel, but he also helped a handful of drivers who felt they didn't have the appropriate vehicle or the skills to cross it on their own. They'd ask my dad to cross it for them and my father never once said no or thought: "shit, what if I make a mistake or what if the current is too strong for this particular type of car…?" Nope, he wouldn't even think about it.

So many variables and I was mesmerized and befuddled by his brave and inconsequent thought process.

"What is he thinking? Is he really doing this, not once but a half a dozen times?" I was watching Indiana Jones in the making.

From truck drivers on a tight schedule, to midsized automobiles, he crossed everyone who asked him and never hesitated for a second or doubted he'd get to the other side…and he did, each and every time.

That was my father, a man who would drive us in the most treacherous roads and rarely banged the bottom of his cars on rocks or rough terrain. He had Mario Andretti's skills on dirt and lack common sense on earth. By the way, he loved Mario Andretti and those old racing gizzards like Emerson Fittipaldi, Nikki Lauda, Alan Prost and Airton Sena.

Once we all crossed the bridge (pedestrians could cross via a pedestrian bridge built above the highway), we realized that we were entering a thick and vast forest which we would have to find a place to sleep and let the car engine and seats dry out to continue our journey to Porto Velho since we still had 2500 kilometers of muddy dirt roads to go. The size of the rivers around this area is something else altogether and one needs to be there to fully understand the magnitude of these massive body of waters which keeps that entire region alive and thriving…till now!!!

A few hundred kilometers later we found a little shack and truck stop with some big diesel Mercedez Benz 18 wheelers parked in front of it. My father thought we should play our luck. He told us to stay in the car while he was going to check out the place. Keep in mind there are three young women and three small children in the car, and we are in the middle of God knows where a few hundred kilometers from anything and anyone in the middle of the Amazon forest. My father got out of the car and started walking towards the shack where we could see a billiard table outside on the front porch and a few men playing with a beer in one hand, a billiard stick in the other and a smoke in the corner of their mouths. It was like I was living inside a Clint Eastwood western flick which my father loved to watch.

It had been raining cats and dogs and the heavy trucks that supply the region with merchandise and trade, they were all stuck because the roads ahead were too dangerous, and you needed to have multiple sets of tire chains to make it thru the mud in certain areas. Some of these trucks/transportation companies would have a flat bed with a tractor to get their trucks off the mud when they'd get stuck. And since we were all on the same boat/road/mud/fucking mess, we help each other out and my father would drive and fix trucks and we would get our little Ford Corcel out of the mud and towed along the way when we'd get stuck which happened three to five times daily for eleven days in a roll. Our journey was supposed to take three days and it took us eleven days of pure hell driving and living in the middle of the Amazon Forest inside a two-door Ford Corcel with five kids, a sick puppy barfing and pooping as if we were traveling in a sailboat in the Bering Sea during crab season.

When my father returned from the funky looking truck stop, he said that there were only men inside the place besides a few native looking dancers as he explained it (hookers) and a few other strange men dressed in all black clothing with black shoes and black hats. It was a truck stop, a brothel, a place where deals were being made because those men dressed in black had no reason to be in the middle of the Amazon unless something shady was going on. They told my father that he could have one room with an outdoor shower which, it wasn't really an outdoor shower but rather a bucket with holes on the bottom hanging above the door with a hose attached to it. I never thought I'd say this, but I was all of a sudden missing the soon to be electrocuted, exposed wires and either too hot or too cold showerhead at our old home in Goiania. We never know how good you have it till you lose it, or perhaps my standards were so low that anything less than being shocked daily wasn't good enough anymore.

The room offered would be almost too small for two people, but my father decided that Nida, my youngest brother Sergio, Tata and Moema, would sleep in that room and me and Cesar would sleep in the car with our dog Zippy who had been vomiting since the flooded bridge cross about 300 km back. As for my father, he would be roaming from the room to the car and back again while entertaining himself with the mischiefs in that joint.

We didn't like the idea very much but we didn't have much of a choice because he couldn't stay with the boys and let the ladies and a baby sleep in a shack type of a room in the middle of nowhere in the Amazon forest by themselves with a bunch of strange looking men, who have been on the road for weeks and months and are feeling lonely, homesick, stressed, concerned for their cargo and fucking horny…nope, let's agree to disagree here but that was the right choice. Fuck the boys, and if we were to be taken and eaten by the variety of predators in the Amazon or kidnapped by some truck drivers or some weirdos dressed in black suits in the middle a muddy forest, oh well, there were too many of us anyways. In the back of my mind, I always thought my father was looking for the opportunity to get rid of some of the liability.

He told us not to worry, he would come and check on us in the middle of the night and that he was going to stay awake and have a beer, play pool and he'd come back periodically thru out the night to make sure we were alright. Great, what a perfect setting; a pool table, alcohol, cigarettes, prostitutes, and some idiots he could hustle and get some money out of in the pool table…let's just hope he doesn't get killed here but wait a minute! My father getting killed in the middle of the Amazon forest may not be a terrible outcome, come to think of it…that was my thinking and yes, I own it.

Myself? The eight-year-old me just sat on the driver seat of that Ford Corcel and let my mind wonder about driving off with my brother and Zippy and never looking back. I was dreaming and feeling like I was in charge. In charge of my life with no one else to tell me what to do. I thought it was my chance to escape and never return but then I realized I had no keys and what to do with my brother and Zippy? Damn, why can't I ever get a fucking break?

At least I was able to feel what it was like to be behind the steering wheel of a car. My brother Cesar sat next to me on the passenger seat and Zippy laid down in the back seat which was cramp with a bunch of things and still wet from the water crossing a few hours ago. I noticed Zippy whining and moving to the wet floor mats behind the driver's seat where I could smell the stench of his wet skin and hear him shiver of cold…I wasn't cold but to be fair, I don't really feel cold most of the time, even when is cold out for most people.

I imagined driving that black 1969 Ford Corcel, completely wet and stinky from dog waste and mildew from the bridge crossing, thru the forest and getting thru some of those difficult patches of road where mud and heavy rain would force folks to change plans but in my thoughts I'd be sliding that Ford Corcel to the right and to the left like I have seen on rally races and mud would splash everywhere but I would get it thru just like my father did on that bridge. I'd be imagining getting thru and getting out of my car and getting inside other people's cars and driving their vehicles thru it and how happy and grateful they would be to me…I could charge them a fee for it, make some dough in the process. I fell asleep while dreaming about driving away, and I thought I was dreaming when my father knocked on the window and woke me up to check on us in the middle of the night. He noticed how Zippy was whining and vomiting inside the car so he put him outside and tied him under the muffler so he could be protected from the heavy Amazon rain and sleep under the car. It felt like a nightmare and not a dream but, nevertheless, that was what we had for that moment in time.

"Shit, if I only had escaped when I had a chance!" I thought.

Not long after that, my four-year-old brother Cesar woke me up and wanted to go pee, it was still dark when I opened my eyes hearing him crying and saying he was afraid to go by himself. I slowly opened the driver door which by this time was stuck with all the mud and humidity and I noticed how dark and beautiful the Amazon forest can be at night even though so many challenges were thrown our way during this journey, and we still had so much distance to go. When we stepped outside, I didn't pay attention if Zippy was still there, but I saw his leash tied to the muffler and assumed he was under the car shielding from the Amazon dark and wet night. We both peed behind the car, stretched our skinny legs and bony bodies and I could hear the men talking around the pool table from a distance, they were arguing and shouting and all of a sudden; bang, bang, bang…three-gun shots were fired, and we rushed back to the car, locked the doors spooked by the loud noise while shivering in complete fear.

I then saw the three men in black clothes running to their pick-up truck and speeding away while my brother cried and put his face against the back of the passenger seat in complete fear.

In my mind I had already created the scenario which I had seen it before with my own eyes; my father was playing pool, having his beer and a few shots of cachaça while puffing on his cigarettes and charming everyone around like he's done it so many times. He would get to a pool table full of unknown wannabe players, bet money and sandbag a few rounds till they wanted to increase their bets only to double or triple up later and he'd clean up the table, arguments and fights would ensue, and he would walk away with all the cash...a true hustler!

A few seconds after the shots, I saw my father, Nida carrying my baby brother Sergio and my sisters running towards the car in the middle of the night, now with rain falling hard again. Everyone scooted themselves inside the cramped Ford Corcel and my dad took off like he was running from a pack of hungry wolves. We couldn't see much in front of us due to the pitch-black night and heavy rain hitting the windshield.

"Stop, stop," I screamed. "Stop, Zippy, Zippy." My father stepped out of the car and we could hear the rain forest with all its might, its beauty and its creepiness, a sound that still lives in my head and the reason I often travel on my motorcycle these days to remote areas of the world, searching for hots springs, waterfalls, nature and two trees to hang a hammock on and watch the beauty of the dark nights and hear the sounds of silence, as if I was waiting for prey like my father used to during his hunting adventures. The rain forest and that insanely crazy adventure, the loneliness of that night, the heavy sounds of the rain, the rustling of the trees and its leaves, the deep shade of those dark nights and the unforgettable chorus of the night creatures in the jungle which I have always called the sounds of silence...I miss it.

My dad came back to the car, slam the door in such a manner that the tiny Ford Corcel shook for a few seconds as if an Amazon gorilla was trying to shake us out. Any time my dad was afraid or upset, which was more often than I care to remember, I hoped he wasn't near any doors because he'd slam the fuck out of it and we could see his blue eyes bulging and protruding out of its socket, his neck getting red and ready to explode with all the blood rushing thru the thick veins, and with a look of desperation on his face, scary to say the least and most definitely, not a welcoming sight.

Zippy was gone, the leash was still hanging on the muffler, but our pooch was nowhere to be found.

In an apparent swift and fearless move, my father turned the car around and went back to the truck stop which wasn't too far from where we were. There wasn't anybody inside since the gunshots, people split for their lives except for an old man who owned the place and told my father, amongst many different things, that gunshots were a daily routine in that part of the world.

"Everything gets resolved with bullets and death in this wretched and forsaken place mister." Says the old man chewing on coca leaves.

"Have you seen a black and white chihuahua around?" Asked my father.

"Mister, dogs and cats and small creatures left outside won't survive for long in this jungle. Too many night predators roam around and prey on small animals and if you left your pooch outside for a minute, the Boa's are everywhere. These giant snakes simply move around too swiftly and quietly to be noticed. I am afraid to break the news to you, but your dog is gone, and you should be too." Said the old man now sipping on some hot tea from a coconut husk shell.

The vibe was heavy inside the car, we were apprehensive about Zippy's whereabouts and weren't sure if the shots a few minutes ago had anything to do with our father.

"Was my father involved? Was he the one been shot at for taking people's money on the pool table? Or was he the one using his 22 caliber Beretta?" I had all these questions running thru my mind without any plausible answer.

We had left in a hurry from that macabre place, and everyone neglected to untie Zippy from the muffler, but we didn't know what transpired, if he was already gone when we left in a hurry or else. Also, who was the fucking shooter? I knew my father was a great shot, we heard numerous stories from him and his friends about wild hunting adventures where he'd shoot his prey from afar and in the dark and he'd rarely missed. He's gone in numerous backpacking hunting expeditions with his friends around the country during his truck driving days, sleeping, and shooting from hammocks from 40 feet high treetops and he always brought back his hunt along with beautiful stories which would soothe me to sleep sometimes. He'd often shared those stories by the riverbank around a campfire at the Araguaia River trips every summer.

The rain was torrential, my father was still inside searching for Zippy and I noticed a shadow of what appeared to be an older lady walking in the dark with a basket over her head and some tapioca roots still covered with mud. I jumped out of the car while my sisters were screaming at me not to do it, and I asked the lady if she had seen a black and white chihuahua.

"Ma'am, I am looking for my dog, a little black and white chihuahua, have you seen it?" I asked

"Ooohhh young man, you shouldn't be outside, it's dark out, very wet and the boas are out and hungry. Sorry about your pup but no I haven't seen it." The old lady replied

She was a beautiful older native, a lonely Amazonian native digging for food in the middle of the night to feed her small family who lived not too far from the truck stop.

I couldn't stop crying, I couldn't go back to that car and continue on that treacherous journey with the possibility that Zippy could be alive and alone in the forest. That was one of the few times in my life I wanted to be dead, I didn't want to continue living anymore, Zippy was my refuge, my best friend and the only one who knew about my dreams, my aspirations, the reason I stared at the ceiling for hours on end, he knew my plans to escape, he knew my secrets, he knew my pain and my sorrows. That night was one which I'd do anything to have changed the outcome for I didn't have anything left in me to keep moving forward. I was eight years old and felt like going on eighty.

CHAPTER VI
Nothing Left in The Tank

We couldn't believe that our puppy was gone, it felt like one of us had died and that we were terrible people for carrying on and not have kept looking for him and bring him home... what home? Our house was rented already to a Christian family who'd go to church almost every night and had bible study twice a week. For an eight-year-old, my mind was already preoccupied with adult things and so many random crap like: Are these people going to pay the rent with that much time spent at church? When do they go to work? The answer was obvious, they were for sure expecting God to provide and now we are venturing into a wild side of the Amazon forest and again with so much uncertainty and absolutely nothing else to lose...so I thought.

I cried all the time because we were told Zippy was eaten by a snake and the possibility that he may still be alive and looking for us made me feel depressed and sad. Maybe he got spooked for having to stay outside and tied to the muffler in the middle of a rainy night in the Amazon forest and escaped into the darkness and ran away looking for a better life, just like we were. Maybe he ran away to hide from wild cats, big monkeys, foxes, crocodiles, and ginormous snakes. What if he comes back to where we were and don't find us there? What would he think of us? Truth is Zippy didn't think much about us anyhow. We were totally messed up, fucked up people trying to be a family with too many mouth to feed and not enough to go around and now with one more mouth on his way, broke without a penny to our names and stupid enough to tie a dog outside onto the muffler of a 1969 Ford Corcel in the middle of the night, right in the smack middle of the fucking Amazon Rain Forest, that's who we were; crazy insane and desperate folks who had nothing else to lose except their dog. And we managed to do just that.

The rest of our trip was gloomy and sad with the loss of Zippy and constantly being stuck in deep and nasty mud for hours waiting to get dragged out of the gigantic potholes by a tractor or a friendly tow truck. That routine was wearing our spirits down and some days we would only drive 10 kilometers the entire day and would have to sleep in the car all seven of us because there was no other place to sleep. I don't remember what we ate during the entire trip after the first couple of days, the food we had brought ran out quickly as we were barely prepared for a three-day journey, much less the entire eleven days marathon. The Transamazonica Highway was pure hell of trucks, mud slides, pot holes, bandits, whores, gigantic dog eating fucking snakes, tractors and plenty of hope for desperate folks with nothing else to lose, like us. Hope that we will get to a city sometime soon. Hope that we could sleep in a regular bed. Hope that we would have clean clothes to wear and shower to clean the mud from our hair, body, and soul. Hope that we could stitch our spirits back together and feel like humans again, hope to just be a kid, play soccer, fly kites and run wild. Hope that we would eventually use a toilet with toilet paper instead of a tree leaf and never squat behind snake infested bushes or into a bucket again. Hope that we would have a normal life like some of our cousins and friends had. Hope that we would go back to school and even get spanked by aunty Nair for crying, if necessary, that seemed better than all this crazy adventure we had embarked on...but it wasn't.

I miss the smell of termite infested wood benches in the main church hall across from serial killer Antonio's barber shop and the moldy impregnated small classrooms inside Sunday school, that was better than the fucking humid and wet weather, the giant mosquitos eating us alive, the stench of dog waste, wet seats and dirty clothes and bodies inside that 1969 Ford Corcel for eleven long days in a wet and humid jungle with no end in sight. There were times I hoped that we would just perish and die already, perhaps a Boa Constrictor could put an end to our existence, this miserable, desperate, and senseless life we were living...now without Zippy. What the hell are we doing? Just when I thought things were about to improve the sense of hopelessness hit me hard and I didn't even have a bed to lay down and a ceiling to stare at, and yet...I even missed the Bayer mosquito spray...FUUUUUUUCK!

"Perhaps Zippy wasn't eaten by a snake after all, maybe he simply ran away, took his chances, and fucking ran away from us, from this crazy life we had imposed on him. Perhaps he learned from me and my ideas about escaping and executed on my plan the first chance he had." My thoughts were running wild.

Somehow, someway we made it through the worst part of the Transamazonica highway and eventually all the way to Porto Velho where perhaps a brand-new Zippy-less life filled with new and better adventures was waiting for us.

My father went straight to work at this mechanic shop he had started with my uncle; his sister's husband Euripedes, the same uncle he bought the Ford Corcel from. Aunt Ana, my dad's younger sister was the rich one in the family, well…she married rich. They lived in a fancy house, drove fancy cars, had expensive clothes and they all had lush hair, possess the best camping gear and always wore very nice shoes. They were charming, fucking great looking rich people which made me envious of them. They were intelligent and interesting people whom I gawked over with every opportunity we spend time with them. Sometimes they would stop by our home in Goiania and bring us food, used clothes, some of the cool old shoes and I was always in awe of their good looks and things they owned. We kids, or maybe just me, would be completely mesmerized by their expensive cars, their rich smell and the way they talked, acted and behaved, like very rich people that they were. I guess my standards were so low and anyone who had anything better than us, which was common, I'd be very impressed with.

Euripedes Junior was their oldest son, a tall, dark haired, and elegant man who my sisters would be gawking over when he showed up at the house. Lilo was the next in line, probably the best looking of all of them and without a doubt one of the most beautiful man I have ever seen in my life. His hair was dirty blond, and he had a big smile with perfect teeth, a smile that would get him anything he ever wanted in life…he got Parkinson's disease today and he can't barely speak, talk and eat on his own. When I saw him last time, I couldn't believe how a healthy and beautiful man like that could have been in such demise. Lilinho was the next one, probably the most charming of them all and a very astute businessman who would always be getting into deals or seemed to be getting out of one. He and his brother Euripedes Jr. used to take math lessons from my mother I learned later. Lilinho and I became close during his passage thru Hawaii where he lived for a few months with his 5th wife Karla (ex-wife now). Lilinho had more wives than I could count. He got married five times and has seven kids amongst them all and I don't' think he's done. Iraima is the only girl of the bunch and looked just like her mom aunt Ana; sensual, sexy, smelled like expensive fragrance all the time and was very soft spoken. Euler was the youngest, a blond kid who never really cared to hang out with us at all, he was too rich and too good for us, and we didn't really give two shits about him either, he was too young and a fucking snob.

My father started this business with the hopes that this was his ticket to a much better life. He worked hard, from early in the morning to late at night every day of the week and weekends, we didn't get to see much of dad during our time in Porto Velho but we were ok with that. We were adapting to this new city, new school, and new life. We had all been enrolled in school and my sisters' made friends with our neighbor next door. I could hear the girls talking about boys, and which one they had a crush on.

We lived in a very modest home in downtown Porto Velho. The house looked like a long hallway that someone randomly decided to put a fucking roof on. It was a narrow lot, with a narrow and steep driveway and the house consisted of a small kitchen at the south lower side of the lot, a tiny living room which wasn't big enough for a couch and a dining table and there was this very large room where we made into our bedroom for all five of us children. We were all bunched up in the same room in bunk beds and my father and Nida had the other room which we needed to get thru to get to ours. We all shared one bathroom, again but at least there was a shower curtain, toilet cover and the showerhead weren't like a death sentence, we could switch from "winter to summer" mode in the humid and muggy Porto Velho weather without frying our asses in the process…horay, progress at last! So I thought.

The property had a very steep driveway and on the rainy days, which was a daily occurrence in this part of the country, the bottom of the driveway would be completely flooded, and the water would get into our kitchen and the small living room located in the lower side of the lot.

On rainy days we missed our lives in Goiania because this place would get flooded so bad and had mosquitos that were so big and noisy, we thought they were fucking birds. That house was also haunted, we were sure there were ghosts in that place and every night we'd hear the spookiest sounds coming from everywhere. It turned out the creepy sounds were bats who hung on the ceramic tile ceiling all over the house and they sounded so loud we had to keep our pillows on top of our faces to cover our ears, otherwise it was practically impossible to sleep. For Christ sake, I was missing the mosquitos in Goiania now and how could it get worse? But it did.

The humidity was difficult to live with because you'd take a shower and change your clothes and in a few minutes be completely soaked due to the high humidity of the Amazon Forest. Needless to say, there was no air conditioning, and the heat was unbearable. A different place, a different city, a different school, different friends and different weather but things were exactly the same, actually it felt worse…fuck me!

My father continued to be a brute and although we were doing better financially because there was always good food on the table and even apples and tangerines which for me, was a signed of wealth since we would never have apples and tangerines in Goiania unless it was a very special occasion, like Christmas for instance.

My sisters Moema and Marta were doing better I thought. They were going through their teenage years and the hormones were raging and with that they made lots of friends, especially with our next-door neighbors and they seemed to be adapting better than me and Cesar. I remember the school I went to in Porto Velho, it was a huge open field of nothingness really and a few red brick classrooms that were so hot, no one could ever learn anything inside those chambers of hell except to plan how to escape. I was not very happy with the school situation and even though I was hoping things would have to get better, I just didn't believe I could last much longer there.

After couple of months, my stepmother Nida had to go to Goiania to give birth because there were no good hospitals in Porto Velho to give birth to Sandro, my 7th sibling. She stayed in Goiania for a couple months before she returned to Porto Velho, my father's partnership with my uncle started to fall apart and the only thing I remember was the death threats my father would be shouting to my uncle as they split up. Things were going from bad to worse and the mood inside the house was getting tense and even though we were leaving in a different city, different schools, different climate, our troubles were all the same.

"Wherever you go, there you are, and you get there, you just arrived." Which to me only meant one thing; no matter where we went, we brought ourselves with us, we brought our problems, our insecurities, our poverty, our emotional baggage, and all of our troubles to the Amazon and the illusion that by moving things would get better, was just that, an illusion because we were the same people with the very same issues and the changes needed were much bigger than just moving somewhere else, the changes needed were in our roots, in our attitude and resolve and not just a change of scenery. We also needed to catch a break somewhere somehow and that break never came.

My father was desperate and seemed to have gotten to the bottom of the pit without any tools to dig himself out. Our lives were in limbo with seven young children, without any money, my father without a job and a failed partnership, without a roof over our heads, without Nida who was in Goiania giving birth yet to another child – Sandro – and without any prospects of where our next meal was going to come from. In June 26, 1974, my dad wrote a desperate letter to Nida explaining that we were finished, he got screwed by my uncle and he needed help, Nida's help to think what to do next because he was out of ideas and wrote about "if he was going to lose everything, he was going to go to extreme measures."

When a man like my father talks about extreme measures, one better be prepared for a wild roller coaster ride because he was desperate, broke, hopeless, confused, hurt, betrayed, lonely, sad, depressed, drunk, and probably suicidal although I never heard him talking about taking his life.

I am not sure what extreme measures meant for my father but I can only imagine his level of desperation and disappointment with my uncle and the promise of a better life in the Amazon. My father was capable of doing everything and anything to survive and as children, we didn't know how far he would go to "make things right" with his brother in law uncle Euripedes.

Porto Velho 26 de Junho de 1974.

Vida espero que você esteje bem com os nossos filhos.

Aqui tudo vai bem a não forre as decepções e incertezas, pois eu não sei o que vou fazer de minha vida de agora para a frente pois fizeram de mim um trampalião mi pegaram para burro de carga e me deixaram na chapada.

Meu bem não, apavore com o que estou lhe escrevendo, eu tenho espírito elevado graças a Deus, e fa esperança pois isso.

Vida eu estou a 15 dias tentando falar com você e não consigo eu não sei porque você não preocupa com nossos problemas e eu não estou dando conta de pensar sozinho. pois a eminencia ca de prefeitura com esta vinda para Porto Velho não tem tamanho e se eu voltar para Goiânia é maior.

Aqui tenho fé em Deus que não vai ficar assim. pois se foi para tomar Prefeitura eu vou ao extremo.

Vire

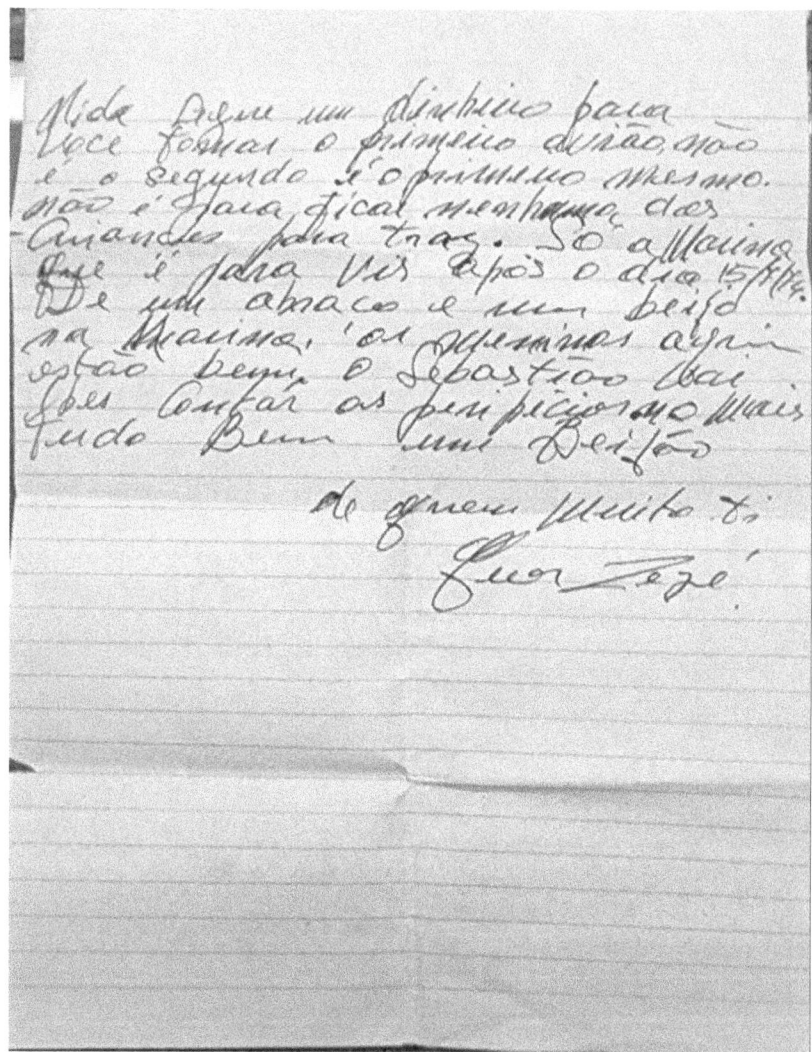

Letter of despair my father wrote to Nida

Since my uncle was the one who put up the money to start the business, my father had to find work elsewhere and now with six children to take care of, another one on the way soon and no money and no job in the middle of a rain forest without many resources, one must return to a familiar environment, but the odds were stacked up against us. All the employees my father recruited from his old mechanic shop in Goiania had been getting their way around town and putting their footprint around Porto Velho. My sisters had made new friends, shit…what now?

We went back to Goiania, my father made a deal with uncle Euripides and our travel expenses were paid and this time we traveled by airplane, which was super exciting for us kids because we had never been on an airplane before and that was a treat. My uncle Euripedes agreed to pay our plane tickets back to Goiania which was the fastest way to get rid of us and the threats and fights him and my old man were having. My father stayed behind to get his Ford Corcel and our furniture and Whatever else we had and send it back to Goiania. It was sad, happy, and confusing to leave because even though I didn't like that place, at least my father was making a decent living, we had good food and even them apples and tangerines on a daily and things were improving slowly...now what?

The plane ride back to Goiania was only three hours and we felt like we were the famous people we'd see on the soap operas with flight attendants serving us sandwiches, sodas, and crackers. We could see from the window seats which we all took turns to spend some time in, the gigantic Amazon Forest from above and it mesmerized me how can we be flying over this forest when just seven months ago we were stuck on its mud and having our dog eaten by it. Poor Zippy might still be there, barking, barfing and looking for us, hopefully he found a better family to be with and was able to avoid the boa constrictors.

The Amazon Rain Forest is simply the most beautiful and most stunning place on the planet and the thought of burning it down at a pace of a few dozen football fields every day, it sickens me and makes me think that we humans have absolutely no fucking idea about anything. How can you burn and destroy your own lungs?

When we arrived in Goiania, we had to spread out to some of our aunties and family members for a while because our home had been rented and we didn't have a place to go to. My father was able to use a tiny house owned by my mom's brother Joao Faria but it didn't fit all of us. I went to my aunt Joana's with my brother Cesar and middle sister Moema. Marta, Sergio and Sandro stayed with my father and Nida at Uncle Joao's tiny home thirty minutes away from the rest of the clan. We would go visit on the weekends and that was a lot of fun because right across the street from the corner house, there was a community pool, and a regulation size green soccer field that I dreamt playing there one day. I would watch from the outside peeping through the trees and bushes that fenced the field, all the men playing with their fancy team uniforms and soccer shoes, high socks, and brand-new soccer balls…that was sweet music to my ears. My father lived in this neighborhood for one year and I was never able to get inside that community club and swim or kick a soccer ball around. That was so frustrating because that place and those people didn't seem rich or anything like that but, the truth is, compared to where we were, everyone were better off. So much for a kid's dream, it seemed simple to just had a chance to play soccer there, but I realized later that one needed to be a member of the club and pay a monthly membership to swim and play soccer and we barely had enough money to eat, much less splurge on swimming and soccer privileges.

On Friday's my father would stop by Auntie Joana's place and pick us up to spend the weekends together. He would ask us kids to pluck his gray hair from his head and he would pay us .50 cents for each gray hair…he would pay us when he'd get rich, of course. We would fight to pluck his gray hair because we too needed some money, but he never paid us a penny, and he never got rich. He was driving a cab again he leased from one of his friends and it felt familiar even though our family was separated.

Us kids were relentless little fuckers though; we would sell anything to have some cash to buy some treats occasionally. Kettle corn was my favorite one, because it would come in a pink transparent small plastic bag and there was always a small "surprise jewel" treat in the bottom of the bag with different types and colors of "diamonds" glued to a metal ring. Sweet heaven!!

The weekdays were about going to school (now at Instituto de Educacao de Goias) and waiting for the weekend to arrive so we could see our siblings and our parents. Marina was still living with Aunt Cro in downtown and she had it better than most of us. Although our aunt and uncle were stingy and accumulated all kinds of old trinkets in their apartment, at least they were well off. They had plenty of good food, and we were a little jealous of Marina's living situation because we had to share everything with our cousins who didn't have enough themselves, but we made due with what we had and since having very little was all we knew, it made no difference to us anymore, except when we'd go visit Marina in downtown. That's when we knew how poor we were and how deprived we had been. At Aunt Cro's apartment there were fruits for breakfast: bananas, mangos, apples and tangerines and honey. They had warm and fresh cakes, different types of breads, fresh milk, fruit juices like guava, passion fruit, fresh homemade cheese and the most delicious butter they'd bring from the farm they owned nearby. They also had all kinds of meats like bacon, steaks, and pork sausages. In our minds only rich people ate like that and rich they were, they had three cars in their garage, a big apartment which could fit them, us and all of the useless shit they accumulated and hoarded inside their place, and yes, they had plenty of money in the bank according to my father.

At Aunt Joana's, our breakfast was comprised of half a glass of milk and a piece of delicious homemade corn bread. For lunch we had rice, beans and tapioca and ground beef stew, and sometimes some chicken or ground beef with potatoes for dinner, but most of the time it was a soup with all the lunch scraps, humble but yummy, nevertheless. We were grateful to them for taking us in while we waited for our house to vacate from the religious renters and we never complained about anything, and perhaps that humble living taught us the importance of being frugal, eating small portions, living in small quarters, and sharing everything with everyone. I think that type of upbringing made us very strong people and even though I feel very privileged today by living in a big house and having the ability to provide so much more to my three children, I can easily survive and feel contentment with a cup of soup, a piece of bread and a mug of hot mate. It seemed like yesterday when we practically felt like there was nothing left in our lives, no gas left in the tank really; no mother, a difficult father who worked like a horse all the time just to get by. Tight and cramped living conditions everywhere we went and yet, we all made it and today we all have so much more than we ever dreamt of.

Sometimes I have this naïve feeling and the poetic and nostalgic thought that life works out for everyone just like the way it worked out for me and my family. We have plenty of challenges and obstacles for sure, but we all have graduated from college, we all had and still have more opportunities than we ever thought we would, and my entire family are comprised of intelligent, healthy, kind, happy and generous people who give and give and give…and we have received hundreds of times more in return.

I said a naïve and poetic feeling because I believe that life doesn't work out for a lot of people, in fact life doesn't really work out for the great majority of people. Plenty of very deprived and generous people don't seem to have the chances to get out of poverty and escape the survival mode and shift into the ever so elusive thriving mode. I pray often for these people and teach my kids to pray by showing them that we ought to be thankful and grateful but more importantly, we ought to be aware that billions of people don't know where their next meal is coming from, where they are going to sleep and where and how to use a toilet with running and treated water, much less a nice and warm shower even with the prospects of frying your ass in the process.

I often think about the more than half a million kids who die in developing nations of diarrhea before they get to be five years of age. They die mainly because they don't have treated water. They defecate and urinate in the same water where they bathe in and drink from. They don't have a sewage system to treat their latrine waste and they die from diarrhea more often than any other diseases. For us in the Western world, when was the last time we have heard of people dying from diarrhea? I have never, because we can always go to the pharmacy in the corner and buy some cheap medication to take care of it and our water is clean and treated, (tell that to the folks in Flynt, Michigan or Red Hill in Honolulu), our sewage is under ground and our water processing infrastructure treat our waste water in ways the water can be reused…so have we been told.

I have, for the last three and a half years been taking cold showers at the beach. Yes, I have seven bathrooms and hot showers in my big house overlooking Diamond Head crater, with gorgeous ocean and the beautiful Honolulu skylight views, but I take a cold shower at the beach. I guess you can take a man out of poverty, but poverty never leaves him. These cold showers are good for me, for my mind and soul and it feels right and refreshing even in the chilly Hawaiian windy nights. I also enjoy when Isabela, my only daughter, joins me from time to time and I can see how much she appreciates all the perks we have. Cold showers help me to relax under pressure and stay calm in moments of agony. Cold showers remind me of how deprived I once was and how much I have now, how privileged I have been, how many opportunities I have been afforded and how many more still to come. Cold showers remind me that most of our world population doesn't even have potable drinking water, much less cold clean water to bathe in, even it is at a public park.

I don't think about how cold the water is at the beach showers or the chilly waterfalls I often seek during my motorcycle trips, instead I jump right in, and I give it no power over my mind. I simply put my neck right under the cold water and let my nerve system acclimate and adapt to the new temperature and after just a few seconds, the water temperature is no longer the focal point, the experience is, the feeling that we are all in this together becomes more eminent even though I know that my showers do not solve the world's problems and the lack of sanitation in poor and developing countries where children die by the millions every year for the lack of clean water and basic necessities. I feel blessed.

CHAPTER VII
Blue Eyes Thru The Window

In the summer of 1974, we returned to our home in Goiania. The religious tenants have gotten divorced, and their lives were a mess, just like the lives of the other non-followers about to move back into their own house: us. We didn't care, it was nice to be home and have our bedroom back even if there were going to be five of us in it. Life was normalizing again since we were all desensitized of the conditions we lived under, and all of us were living under the same roof with my father and Nida, including Marina who left her cushy life in downtown to be with us. Now we were a gang of eight kids and two adults, and even though my father was still the same harsh and cruel man, life was getting back to normal regardless if the craziness never subsided in our home.

I got enrolled at Colegio Lyceu de Goiania; a good school and one where plenty of kids in that part of town wanted to go to. However, the challenge was the distance. The school was a good 2.5 km track away from the house and we never got a penny for bus or a car ride from my father; we walked to school every day. None of my siblings were going to the same school though, which was so far away, but somehow, I ended up there and they were the best and worst years of my life.

To begin with; the walk was dreadful, uphill under the extreme hot dry weather in Goiania. The air is so dry that the inside walls of my nose would get all crusty and bloody on a daily basis. To this day, Goiania still feels too uncomfortable for me and my visits there are usually for just a couple of days, and I am gone to some waterfall in the south or my sister's farm forty-five minutes away from the city.

I attended school in the morning, so I had to leave the house around seven am to get there before eight when the school session started. We would have a gathering in the school's front lawn and then we sing the national anthem and couple of other feel good and protect your nation type of songs…and to the classroom we'd go.

Our classrooms were on the shady side of the building and that was a break from the walk to school and the walk back at around 12:30PM, when you could literately fry a fucking egg on the hot asphalt, without a doubt. When it rained, we could see the steam coming off from the pavement and it would get even hotter with all the humidity. Goiania rains often and the combination of rain and dry heat is a funky thing to deal with.

We'd stayed in one classroom and sat in the same chair the entire year and the teachers for each subject rotate every hour into the different grades and classrooms. Usually, we had Math at 8:00 I guess to catch our minds open and in the learning mode while things where still fresh, unless you had to walk for fifty minutes under such an intense heat that not only could fry an egg but it also fried my brain. History/Geography at 9:00, Portuguese at 10:00, a snack break between 11:00 and 11:30 and science between 11:30 and 12:30. Since I had never got any money for snack or a snack box to bring to school and the school didn't offer lunch, I would go thru the entire morning hungry as a motherfucker and food was about the only thing in my mind during those years at Colegio Lyceu. Come to think of it, I think I spent most of my infancy and teen years wishing and dreaming for more food.

With my frame at around to 6 ft. tall, and 90 lbs. of pure bone and skin, this 10-year-old was lacking nutrients and muscles…any kind of muscles. The other kids in school would tease me and say things like: "Lenox is so skinny that he can walk on the rain and not get wet." I had such a huge complex about my body, my hair and my Freddy Mercury bucked teeth that sometimes I wouldn't go places with the fear of being teased and bullied…and teased and bullied I was often, and honestly, that shit made me sad but also gave me tough skin and made me hearty and mentally strong I believe.

Sometimes I would be watching my classmates and friends line up in front of the food truck parked outside to buy the awesome looking pastries. I don't have the slightest fucking clue how those good-looking pastries tasted like, but they looked succulent, and I wanted one so bad. The cheese breads, the chocolates, a cold coke, or guarana soda. I would be salivating, imagining the day when I would show up to school driving my own black six-cylinder Chevy Opala 4100 SS. The day I would have cash in my pocket to buy a snack in school and seat with the boys and feel like I belonged. That dream never came thru while living in Goiania though. So, during snack break I decided to join the other poor kids without money for snacks and play soccer with a ball made out of old socks and newspapers I'd bring in my brown bag. Sometimes we would play soccer for the entire 30-minute lunch break and be all sweaty when we return to the classroom for our last session of the day. By then, my mind couldn't concentrate on anything anymore. My only thought was what am I going to have for lunch at home?

I would pack my stuff from my single school chair all made of wood with a hole on the left side for the pencil and eraser shavings. Right under the table there was a single shelf where we could place our books and note pads. Most of the students had a school bag or a backpack to carry their stuff, I had a brown bag from "Cobal Supermarket" which would last for a few weeks till it'd get wet and completely disintegrate from walking home under one of many Goiania's infamous torrential rains with thunder and lightning storms.

Still, what's for lunch? Could we please have meat today? My prayers would be that some of my siblings wouldn't make it home in time for lunch which was served on the dot at 1PM because that's when my father could take his lunch break from the mechanic shop he was working during the day while taxi driving at night.

White rice, red beans, chayote sautéed with garlic, onions, fried plantains.

"Yes, we got ground beef today, fuck yeah and Moema isn't coming home for lunch…YES!!! There's more for everyone else." That was mine attitude towards food; the less people the better.

I had been functioning from 6:30AM to 1:00PM on a small baguette and a glass of hot matte, I walked 2.5 km to school, went to five classes which I retained nothing, played soccer for thirty minutes, saw some of my friends having a yummy snack with a delicious Guarana soda and tracked the 2.5 km back home on foot under the midday heat of Goiania. When at home I'd eat anything put in front of me and if there was one thing my father and all the women in my family knew and know how to do well, is to make great food with very little. Our food was simple, but we could have rice and beans and it would be fucking gorgeous, always. I guess the secret recipe was to starve people to death and whatever they eat, they will love it. My hunch is my parents taught us how to appreciate the little we had by not having much at all, they didn't plan it that way…it was by default.

The fried plantains were a treat and counted; 2 slices per head if someone was missing for lunch, we would share in equal parts whatever wasn't claimed, same with the meat if we were lucky enough to have any that day. Lunch time was always a tense situation because my father was not very pleasant around the lunch table during the week, except on Sundays, he was his normal brute self, impatient, and demanding. No surprises there!

The table seating was religiously set with my father seating on south end head of the table, I would be to his immediate left, Moema would be to my left, Sergio to her left, Marina on the other head of the rectangular old dining table with bent and broken legs from my father's tossing it around a few times in some of the fights with my mother, stepmother, and my sisters.

Marta to Marina's left, and Cesar would be seating right next to my father. Don't you dare take anybody's spot or you won't hear the end of it. Don't even fucking think about saying anything that could upset my father or share any of your concerns, challenges, problems, bullying and school issues, your grades or lack thereof…nothing, just shut the fuck up and eat your lunch!!! This was his time to exercise his Kingship power and we never dare to challenge it. The table would have to be set before he came home with all the plates facing down, with the fork to the right and knife to the left of each plate, an aluminum cup for my father to drink his water while eating, a plastic blue color jar of cold water immediately in front of him, another jar filled with roasted tapioca flakes (farinha), and a glass jar with red hot "malagueta" spices in olive oil and vinegar.

He would take two of 'em crazy hot malagueta fuckers, smash and brake them down in small pieces with his fork, sprinkle some of the juice made from the olive oil and vinegar and mix the seeds the shell and the juice on the bottom of his plate before he put the red beans on top, dried tapioca flakes on top of the beans, mix the beans and the tapioca flakes, throw couple of spoons of rice on top, one large spoon of chayote, two pieces of fried plantains and if were lucky enough, whatever protein that happened to be on the menu that day…always in that order. He didn't eat much but the man was methodical and disciplined with his food.

My father would take the first bite and we could feel how hot it was from his reaction every single day. He would immediately reach for the water jug and take a big gulp of cold water while spilling half on the table and blaming it on us: "who the fuck filled up this water jug all the way to the brim, how many times I have to tell you not to fill it all the way up?"

And the best and scariest part: he'd choke often, and it happened so frequently that it was like; "oh well, here we go again!"

Nida would be seating on the steps of the kitchen while holding Sandro on her arms and she would stop her eating with her hands routine and run to help my father because his big and deep blue eyes would be bulging out of his eye sockets while his face would get so red, you'd think he was going to explode like one of those Tom & Jerry cartoons. I always thought that it was the hot pepper, but the tapioca flakes made him choke as they expanded with water. He drank the water in one big gulp and the combination of spicy hot "malaguetas" and the tapioca flakes he mixed with his food caused him to choke. Tapioca flakes expand when in contact with water, so, it would block his throat but none of us had the courage to tell the man; "dude, don't put that much "pimenta malagueta" and tapioca flakes on your plate, but even if you do, don't drink any water right away because it will fucking choke you." Nope, don't you dare say anything or he will give you that look that would destroy you without even saying a word, which by the way, he always did have words to say. In fact, he wouldn't say it, he would yell them:

"Nida, Nida, give me another cup of water, where the fuck is the water? Who set up this table and forgot the fucking water?" My father would say daily. Too much, too little, too hot, too cold, there was always something we didn't do right, and we paid dearly for it.

Nida couldn't say, "The water is in front of you but don't drink the water, you will choke on the tapioca flakes." No, she couldn't say anything, even if to save his life, she just had to do what the king demanded and that's it. We didn't mind when he left the table in the middle of lunch, which happened quite often, on his way to the bathroom because now we could talk. That scene was so familiar that nobody cared anymore about his whole choking drama, we knew he was going to end up in the bathroom, the only bathroom we had in the house for all nine of us to share. And honestly, it was a good thing for him to be the first one in the bathroom while we were eating because he took his sweet time on the no seat cover toilet bowl anyways, and we all needed some time for ourselves on the lunch table without all that tension.

We could hear my father walking into the bathroom, slamming the door which, you couldn't lock it unless you stuck your pinky in the small hole and push the broken latch…we could hear everything, and he would make all kinds of noises. The bathroom was just three small flight of stairs away from where we were seating and he had to jump over Nida who was seating on the floor by the kitchen door and run to the toilet. I guess the whole hot pepper and farina thing caused him to have the runs as he would leave the table and go straight to the bathroom which had a high rectangular louver style glass window just above to the left of the dining table where we were seating. The window would only swing open a couple of inches because the handle was broken in half, and, like the bedroom windows, was too heavy and completely rusted to open or shut it close. With my father in the bathroom and away from the table, we would be talking about each other's day, the tasks we each had in the afternoon: Moema will sweep the house, Marta will wash the dishes, Cesar will dry the dishes and Sergio can help put them away in the old blue metal, falling apart roach infested magnetic doors cabinet. Marina will teach piano lessons, Lenox will clean the bathroom…wait, not just clean it, but literately wash the bathroom from top to bottom. Every day was some cleaning to do, and while we'd be talking about our day and divvying up the house chores, my father would be watching and listening attentively thru the window crack above while taking a crap.

I could see from where I was seating his scary and bulging deep blue eyes staring down to where we were seating, the creepiest thing ever.

"How the fuck he gets up that high? The rusty glass louver window is at least six feet above the toilet seat and you can't be that high while seating on that toilet?" Yes, you got it right: he'd be standing on it.

King Zeze Jube - Araguaia River

After lunch we would get onto our chores so we could finish and go play a bit before my father comes home for dinner when all the fun and play and games must cease. I'd prepare my bucket with water and Clorox to throw it on the walls and use a brush on a long stick to wash the tiles from floor to ceiling and when I'd get to the toilet, I would notice my father's shoes imprinted around the ring of the bowl. The man would do his necessities standing up while watching and listening to us chatting away on the dining table down below. Since he was a child, he learned to used latrines made from a hole on the ground where they'd stand and "go to town" on it…He never shook that habit till years later when he was too old to get up on the toilet without falling inside of it. In the ultra-tense days, I wished he'd fall, hit his dense head and drown in that fucking toilet bowl so we could flush him down and be done with his antics. Yes, it would be that bad and the man never really shook that habit till very late in life…perhaps he became afraid of heights.

Every now and then we would hear a loud noise and it would be my father slipping from the edges of the wet toilet bowl and having his foot stuck inside of it. It was pretty ghetto indeed but nothing we could do about it; nobody was astute enough to tell him "Your highness, please don't stand on the damn toilet to take a shit, it's not safe." I was brave but not that stupid.

At school, I was struggling both socially and academically. I had a few friends whom I played soccer with during recess: Joao Carlos, Mauro, Evaristo, Everton, Fernando, to name a few but only Joao Carlos was someone who I spent quality time with. We met each other in our first day of school at Lyceu de Goiania and found out that we lived in the same neighborhood. So, every day, I would wait for Joao Carlos to walk by my house on his way to school se we could walk together and again back home after school except for the days when his older brother Oloriston would give him a ride on his Yamaha DT 180cc motorcycle.

Every now and then we would venture out in getting inside a bus thru the back door without paying but often enough we'd get kicked out and had to finish on foot, or better, on our "Congas or Kichutes." For us and especially for me, those shoes were the best, because that's all we had, especially Kichute. Congas had a few different colors but mostly just a white material wrapping around cheap rubber which I shared with my sisters, or better, they shared theirs with me as it was their shoes and not mine. Because I was so tall and my feet grew very fast, I could wear my older sisters' Congas every now and then, but my feet were growing too fast and outgrowing even my sister's humble white Congas which were too small and started to hurt my feet. Sometimes my toes would be cramped inside those shoes, but it was cool to be able to wear those sneakers I thought. The Kichutes were a different story though; they came in black color only and they were like a hybrid of a walking/soccer shoes with rubber cleats and long black strings. They were made by Alpargatas, the same company who created the infamous "Hawaiianas" slippers. The thing about Kichutes though was they stunk badly, it didn't matter how much I washed and let them dry and washed my feet and wore my father's clean socks and even sprinkled some powder inside, nothing worked. They were made from old tire scraps and remnants of cheap rubber probably lethal for human consumption. They were awesome to wear and terrible to remove from your feet because of the rotten smell, or perhaps it was just me, I don't know.

When I'd come home from school wearing Kichutes, my sisters would put them by the door outside and wouldn't allow me to bring them inside the house, they made me wash, dry and rub my stinky feet with alcohol afterwards to ease the stench which I never blamed them for it, how could I? I couldn't stand the stench myself.

When we played a neighborhood organized soccer match and we had to put the uniforms and socks on by the soccer field, I'd try to be discrete and slip away from the boys because they'd ask where that stench was coming from, and I didn't have the "cahones" to claim it. I was courageous but not an idiot, they would bully me, and I wouldn't hear the end of it. I'd been given more nicknames and been made fun of for years to come and I wasn't about to give them more fodder for their own entertainment…fuck that, I was stinky but not dumb.

I played mid fielder and forward and I was a very good player. Not the best, but a player that didn't jeopardize the team and held the team together with my passes, my grit my passion and my competitiveness. I wasn't the fastest, but I was intelligent and sneaky around the box. I never missed a game, and the team could always count on me even if I had to sneak out of the house against my father's orders. There would be tournaments with teams around our neighborhood and some rivalries were created where I couldn't even walk near the rivals' houses, otherwise they beat the shit out of me just for disrespecting the few blocks of geographical separation. So much for geofencing and social distancing! In those days I had to go around the block and walk twice the distance on my way to the bakery in the morning just to avoid conflict because it was "on" all the time. Specially if our team beat the other team the weekend before…I was sneaky but not physically strong.

That year I had a dream come true; I got a bicycle for Christmas, a blue Tigrao Devil, I couldn't believe it, I must be doing something right I thought. A very cool bluish devil of a bike with two mirrors and a killer red color bell and a little rear seat that wouldn't fit a midget child's ass. I would take that bike everywhere, and my life changed from that point forward. I became addicted to life on two wheels. I couldn't take it to school because my father gave me strict orders not to and it would probably have gotten stolen but except for that, I now had wheels and since that day forward, I have owned a two-wheel toy ever since. I was impressed with Santa Claus and his generosity was a great gesture of how to make a kid happy.

The only problem was that I sometimes would take the bike in the morning to pick up our small baguettes for breakfast and I would be dreaming about one of them pastries displayed on the glass case, and I'd forget to ride the bike back home and only remember about it during a boring math class when I'd be seating in my classroom at school a few kilometers away and hours later. The light would go on in my head and I'd remember I didn't ride my bike back home from the bakery. Math was my first class of the day, and I couldn't get out of school and walk two and a half kilometers to go fetch my Tigrao bike.

"Fuck, my father will kill me if he finds out I forgot my bicycle at the bakery." The anxiety would drive me crazy, and I couldn't pay attention to anything at school; what if the bike gets stolen? I wouldn't be able to explain to my father and I'd certainly have to run away for good…not a bad idea and a good excuse to leave I'd thought but, regardless, shit would hit the fan for sure.

Some days I wouldn't remember about the bike at all, and I'd get home from school and my father, whom with a quick glance could see everything around the house, would ask me about my bike and I couldn't tell him where it was because I didn't know till I remembered that I left it at the bakery. What ensued after that was always mortifying to me.

"How can you fucking forget your bicycle at the bakery? You had to walk right in front of it to come home?" My father would question me, puzzled about what to do with me because that type of situation was unprecedented, and it was happening with frequency, it was almost as if he was genuinely concerned about my forgetfulness as a health condition rather than irresponsibility of forgetting the bike he bought me for Christmas with money he didn't have and so much difficulty.

I never had the answers my father was looking for because there was no good explanation as to why I would forget the bike at the bakery, and only at the bakery. I never forgot it anywhere else, but at the bakery it was a constant event and I even asked myself the same question all the time; "why do you forget your bike there Lenox?" The only plausible answer to me was because I literally loved the sweet breads but could never afford them, so when the helper asked for my order, I would tell him:

"Five small baguettes please and, how much is this sweet bread with the shredded coconut on top?" Knowing that I wasn't going to get one perhaps made me forgettable and made me dream about the texture of the dough melting in my mouth, the sweet taste and texture of the shredded coconut on top, and perhaps the inability to buy one and the frustration of being that poor clouded my memory and made me forget the damn bike.

I am and have always been a dreamer, sometimes naively so but I believe dreaming is one of those things that I'll never stop doing, I like to dream, to wonder on the what ifs of life and my dreams sometimes can be seen by others "out of my realm of possibilities." I also believe that dreaming is the beginning of any manifestation process necessary to bring about realization, accomplishments and make life worth living. I tend to cling to my dreams and stubbornly make them into reality eventually.

There were many questions my father and I had about why I'd forget my bicycle at the bakery, but the best explanation I have is that my desire to one day walk into that bakery and buy all the sweet bread I wanted would make my mind wonder and perhaps the neurons would shut my memory off, I don't know for sure. We can get scientific about it and speculate that because of all the trauma at a very young age I developed brain atrophy and research shows that people with brain atrophy, also called cerebral atrophy, lose brain cells (neurons), and connections between their brain cells and brain volume often decreases. This loss of neurons can lead to problems like reasonable thinking, memory loss and performing everyday tasks, and the greater the loss, the more impairment someone has. I don't know for sure but all I know is that even my beloved bluish Tigrao bicycle would fall victim of my forgetfulness and my longing for a simple fucking sweet pastry.

Something happened in my head for sure because it was almost a weekly event and I would never do it on purpose because the fear of losing my bike and being yelled at and called all kinds of denigrating names by my father, was plenty of motivation not to forget the damn bike there…oh well, I will never know the real reason, just like I will never know why my father kept staring at us with those intense set of blue eyes thru that cracked window while standing on the wet toilet bowl…creepy shit (pun intended)!!!

By the time I was 10 years old, I had already lived a full life it seemed like. I felt like my childhood was a blink and becoming a teenager wasn't all that attractive to me except for the possibility of running away one day. Now all I want is to get to tripple digits because I love living and being on two wheels still is my favorite pastime and one that I am very passionate about - with the exception of seeing my children play a tennis match, shape a beautiful surfboard or do a perfect impersonation of Eminem, motorcycles are my passion. I owned plenty of them in my lifetime and currently own two 2012 triple black BMW Adventure and one white and blue 2006 limited edition BMW 1150 GS Adventure and still ride them as often as I possibly can. I don't forget them in front of the bakery however, but I do get the sweet pastries though…they are delicious indeed.

Father, Nida, Marina, Moema, Marta, Lenox, Cesar, Sergio and Sandro. We were all living under the same roof at Rua 217 Vila Nova #11, Goiania-GO 74000. Life was incredibly difficult again and it seemed that with each year things would get more challenging. As I got older, I started to question even more; what was the point of this whole thing called life? Yes, I was 10 years old, and I already had these questions which I still don't have the answers today.

I think the point is to be curious, have family, a partner (maybe) and kids and be forced to learn the things we didn't learn while young and single. Learn to share, learn to break the mode of conditioning and cycles and the habits acquired in infancy via the influence of your elders. Learn not be fearful, learn bravery and courage, learn to be humble, kind, loving and not to say everything you want to say all the time although it feels great to have no filters. There are so many good reasons to be alive, especially when there are other people that we are responsible for, particularly when what you do and what you say can influence the ones you love the most, forever. Well, I am still learning, and I will be learning till the day I die because if I was giving a blank space to define myself in one word, I'd say I am CURIOUS.

When I die, I want my motorcycles to be given to my children so they can explore their own curiosities, enjoy the their own thrills and pleasures and, if they can't ride them, I hope they have a big enough living room to park them inside their homes and remember about their old man thru them, an object that represents freedom in every sense of the way, a toy they can not only transport themselves on but teleport themselves back to me thru their own dreams, the feeling of the wind on their faces, the sweet aroma of flowers and trees, rivers, waterfalls and hot springs. The sensation of rain and dirt all intertwined into one, the insatiable pleasure of riding on a rainy day knowing that the storm will pass, the challenges and obstacles will subside, and the sun will shine again and perhaps be lucky enough to ride towards an elusive end of a rainbow, ideally on an unpaved road.

That's what motorcycles represent to me; curiosity for life, curiosity for the unknown and an excuse to never be satisfied with the circumstances we have been handed. I can easily explain my love for two wheels because it was my salvation, an alchemy to my dysfunctional existence, a way of reinventing myself over and over again, just like a dirt and muddy road is never the same twice.

Way Home

Sometimes words are a nuisance
They sound what we feel
But don't mean what we want

At times our actions are crazy
They don't reflect what we want
But show how we feel
In my days of past I was able to do both:
Sound and act insane
In others just wish to refrain
To be sane, to be tamed...in vain

Time cures all
From afflicted hearts
To the loss of loved ones
It heals the persistent wounds
And time always prevails, always wins

The only real time in this brief life is now
And now is where we ought to live

For life is like a beautiful flower
It won't last forever
It might just be for hours

At times I thought I could live forever
Fight all my inner battles with vigor
Put out the fires with force
Conquer the world

But, Just like flowers do
I got to grow old too
For my day has come
Like all beautiful flowers wither
I too will find my way home.

It seemed to me that the only plausible reason to our existence is that we are here to make a shit load of mistakes and have plenty of stories to tell, a bunch of unbelievable tales to write about and hopefully have a good enough memory to teach and tell others; our kids, our loved ones and ourselves but especially, I think we are here to learn so we can pass on to others the lessons in hopes that we leave this planet better than how we found it.

Marina was already a sophomore at the state University in Goiania with the goal of becoming a doctor. Pretty amazing that someone in our family and social economic class could dream to be a doctor and become one. We didn't have enough room in our lives to dream about much except what, when, where our next meal will come from. Considering our unsurmountable challenges and obstacles, seven of us graduated from college (Sergio is the only one who didn't want to go to college) with various degrees; from Doctors, Business, Architects to Social Worker and everything in between. Being the oldest, Marina set the standard for everyone else; she was disciplined, committed to become a Dermatologist and she did. She played the piano beautifully and taught piano every afternoon during her entire time in college and medical school to support her dreams. We had a few neighbors who took piano lessons from her. Our house was small but a revolving door with many students in and out of it all the time, we didn't have a choice but to hear the loud piano across from the TV room in this other little room we called "sala de visita" (guest room), with parquet wooden floors. The room had glass sliding doors with a few broken glass panels from our soccer playing outside and rusty heavy metal door frames on tracks which could only be open in one side and strictly by my father. These doors stayed locked for the entire year except for Christmas when my dad would open them, and we'd seat outside in our front porch and crack some Brazilian nuts from their hard shell while listening to Julio Iglesias and Benito de Paula. Pretty fucking depressing at that time if you ask me but that's how our Christmas were, and I cried most of the time and could only think about my mother and how much I was missing her and how unfair to not have my mom to share Christmas, those hard nuts and all my troubles with.

I never really cared for Christmas, to me there was always the thought of my mother and it never really felt like happy times, even though my father was usually nice and in a good mood during the holidays. I give him credit because he did make a great effort to make it fun and plentiful food wise. During Christmas he had time off from work and he hangout around the house and it was fun; he would play soccer with us, listen to music, and even play the guitar which he was terrible at it, but he did it anyways. He would tell great fishing stories and hunting tales and the mood was light and joyful. And the food!!! Well, that was the best part of Christmas in my house. Even when the menu was rice, beans, lettuce and tomatoes salad and some small omelet, everything always tasted amazing and to this day all of us talk about it and we all know how to cook and cook well.

At Christmas, the menu would be taken to Anthony Bourdain's standards, and I have never experienced food that good anywhere, even to this day. By far the best food I'd ever eaten in my life, and sadly, even after dinning at two and three stars Michelin restaurants in France, that taste from the food my father and Nida cooked, was the best and will never be replicated. We knew what they put in their recipes, we have all watched hundreds of times how they made chicken casserole, mash potatoes and pasta and yet, none of us can even come close to that perfection.

I have always missed my father's cooking and during his final years, I had the privileged to seat at his kitchen very often and watch him cook, taste his very simple beans and rice to perfection. I can smell the aroma and sense his precise and smooth movements around the small kitchen in the same house where we all grew up in it, I can still feel his presence and smell the onions and the fresh garlic jumping on olive oil inside the old iron cast pan.

Food or lack thereof, was probably what kept us together for so long and keeps us close to this day, we all love our kitchens and talking about food. We share recipes, we brag about who makes the best chicken, who makes the best pasta, the best Pao de Queijo (cheese bread), best beans and lasagna. Often when we get together the conversation revolves around food or bread someone is experimenting with. If my entire family lived in the same city and were to open a restaurant, I know for sure it would have great food because we each can cook creatively and well; from Marina to Saulo, thanks to our parents and specially my father who was the best of them all.

But food, although an important part of our growing up, was also a topic for arguments, discord, and fights because except for some Sundays, Christmas or someone's birthday, as good as it was, there was never enough to go around. I have this theory that my father always starved us so he could brag about his cooking skills because we all wanted to learn how to replicate it, but my hunch is he acquired his reputation of a great cook thru starvation and scarcity and definitely not thru abundance. We were always hungry; I was always hungry…for anything and everything!!!

I would come back from school and go straight to the fridge and grab myself a fresh tomato which we had plenty of it being that it was very inexpensive and readily available. A pinch of salt in hand, I'd climb the guava tree, seat on my favorite branch, and take a big bite on that tomato and lick some salt from the back of my hand, the best taste ever. I've always felt comfort with tomatoes and my first thought was always that I was eating a succulent apple or a sweet persimmon. I craved for apples and have always loved persimmons, but we never really had them at our house; too expensive. Each Sunday when my father would come back from the farmers market, I'd dream about him bringing a bag of apples, but he would bring plenty of apple/persimmon looking tomatoes so, I learned to love tomatoes…still do.

In that rusted, falling apart two wheels man made little groceries cart, my father had to carry his pickings from the farmer's market most

Sundays except for his weekend fishing trips. The usual suspects were fresh corn, potatoes, rice, orange, or tangerines on a special occasion and only when one of them was on sale, never both. There was also a big fresh lettuce head, cucumbers, tapioca root, roasted tapioca flakes (farina), red beans although black beans made the list often because they were cheaper and they lasted longer 'cus we didn't like'em that much, except for feijoada on an eventual birthday Saturday afternoon. If my theory is right, black beans would last longer only because the always hungry kids would eat less of it.

He also brought that infamous free-range chicken (frango caipira). This is no Whole Foods organic and friendly murdered free range, cage free, roaming free bull shit wimpy bird…no sir! This motherfucker would put us kids thru the ringer, the Sunday chicken routine was intense, and these clever birds came from somebody's backyard, and they needed to be caught first before we could eat it. Eventually it'd end up having his neck twisted a few times and broken, its feet tied down, hang upside down on a guava tree and dunked on boiling water, "defeathered" and if that wasn't enough, let's bring this little fella to a blazing fire to clean its dirty feet… all of that, while the bird was still conscious and half alive. Yes, that kind of chicken!!! Talking about fresh food!

Finally, fresh okra and plenty of the apple/persimmons looking tomatoes made their way inside that cart every Sunday and into our small blue fridge in the corner of our tiny kitchen.

CHAPTER VIII
Putting Some Meat On!

By the end of Spring of 1975, we all had jobs and my father was moonlighting as a taxi driver at night and working as a mechanic during the day. Nida was teaching at a nearby school, Marina was teaching piano lessons and making fancy hangers with beautiful lining and selling to friends, family and at the university where she had a pretty good demand for them. Moema had started to visit people at their home with her mobile manicure and pedicure business which was going strong. Tata was making strawberry, pineapple and peach pies and selling them at school and on the streets, to the neighbors and family parties and kicking ass with her sweet treats. I was selling and delivering Marina's hangers, Tata's pies, mangos from the yard and I created my own little business: I decided to make a triangular shoe polish box from some lumber we had in the backyard. It was one of those boxes that had a foot support in front, a little compartment for the "Nugget Shoe Polish Paste," a big and softer brush to polish the shoes with lightning speed, a couple of old tooth brushes for the application on the small areas around the shoes, and a some soft cotton rags which was my favorite part of the job; it required strong but yet, delicate hands to apply the rag in constant left to right and top to bottom motion and give the shoe that shim and final touch my customers were looking for. I acquired my customers usually on Saturdays when I would walk around the neighborhood and as far as my bike would take me with the box hanging on my right shoulder, knock on people's doors and ask them if they need their shoes to be cleaned and polished.

Lenox's Caixa de Engraxate (Shoe Polishing Box)

To my surprise, getting customers was easy because people seemed to love the door service I was providing, and they didn't have to go to the market where there were a few shoes polishing stations they could seat on a highchair and the "engraxates" (shoe polishers) would take care of them. I wasn't charging much because I wanted my customers to love my service and have me back over and over to keep their shoes in good condition.

I loved the work, especially the riding around on my bike with my "engraxate box" hooked on my shoulder facing back, feeling like I could conquer anything I wanted and dreaming that soon enough I would be able to go to the bakery and buy some of them pastries once and for all. Most of the money was managed by my sister Marina though, who'd collect my earnings and put it in a tin can with my name on it. She said that money was for school uniform, shoes and socks and the eventual new clothing for birthday parties, weddings, or a baptism of one of our many cousins.

"What? How about what I want? How about some pastries?" I'd often ask her for my money to no avail.

Our extended family was huge, nine uncles and aunties and their spouses from my mother's side: uncle Pedro, Limirio, Joao, Zezinho, Aunt Maria, Joana, Justine and my mom Isabel. Their respective spouses: Auntie Nair the infamous school principal, aunties Celia, Rosa, Adelia, uncles Ari, Ronol and Joao Cordeiro. With that many uncles and aunties who procreated like rabbits do, there were plenty of cousins and birthday parties almost every weekend. Most of our uncles and aunties appeared to have a little better social economic situation than us. Perhaps it was just an appearance and a perspective from a growing kid who wanted to eat better and more often and dreamt bigger than most. But the reality was they were all better off than we were, they had cars, good looking clothes and nice shoes and never complained about not having enough food.

To attend the family gatherings, depending on the occasion and whose house it was, we had to get new clothing and that cost money, lots of it because any amount of money for us, was more than we could spare. So, we would only attend the more important parties and I often had to have new clothes made. My sisters would go to a dry goods store and buy the material. I'd would get measured from head to toe because I was growing too fast and the last clothe made didn't fit me anymore. I had no choice in what they were buying for me to wear, I would either be wearing something too tight or too short because we couldn't buy enough material and when we did, they were in awful colorful print material because it was on sale, either way, it was never what I liked or thought I was safe from being teased and made fun of when we arrived at those awful parties. When my sisters showed up with the material in whatever cheapest print they chose, I would get measured for it and two days later my new clothing would be ready: a shirt and matching shorts and if the occasion was a little more important, pants which was always a challenge because my waist was very slim, the legs very long and I had absolutely zero ass. Some of the colors and prints they purchase were just not right. I would often think they were literally fucking with me because they'd buy the weirdest prints and colors which didn't match me or any other little kid on the planet but since I didn't have a choice, I just wore that funky stuff they got me and never really complained about it. It was going to be worn just once anyways and I already felt so out of place and so bat-shit ugly anyways that another awful looking outfit wasn't going to make any difference, if there was good food at the party, I wouldn't give two shits about the hideous outfits, the tradeoff for good and plentiful food was too great to bitch about it.

Evidently, when we would get to the event, all nine of us in a cramped up little car, I stood out like a giant freaking bamboo stick amongst midgets and succulents. I was freaking tall, and my hair was always big and messy, my face filled with zits and my arms so long, I could almost scratch my feet without bending. My cousins and uncles would make fun of me and my clothes, of course. These motherfuckers were so mean that they would say "I could lay down on a needle and cover with a thread," that "I could walk on rain and not get wet," that "I could use my hair as an umbrella because no matter how much water it fell on it, it would never get wet," and that "I was the ugliest thing they ever seen." These bastards were what I called my family and It was rough and ruthless and embarrassing for me but funny for them. When I hear about kids being bullying these days, I laugh and think that kids today wouldn't last a day in my neighborhood and my family parties.

I didn't cry about it or fought about it, I took it on the chin, and I was so used to it that it didn't matter anymore. I hated those birthday parties for those reasons and because I always felt inferior, I was always being made fun of and didn't have a choice but to go with the family, but the food was off the hook, so I went along and ate it up, literately and figuratively.

Truth be told, those parties prepared me for the world on my own. My skin became very tough, and I was able to take their jokes and abuse and not react to it, not fight it the way they wanted me to fight it. I fought it my way; I went to work, I dreamt about making money and transforming my body one day in an athletic one. I dreamt about leaving that town forever and never return and leave all those motherfuckers behind and one day come back to visit and have my own car, a place of my own and a telephone with an answer machine with a mile long chord so I could walk around my place while talking to important people perhaps. I wanted to rub my success on their faces...my attitude was "fuck these idiots."

I started to make my personal goal to go to these parties dressed up like a clown, it was going to be the case regardless, might as well take advantage of the awesome spread they always had. Plenty of dishes we would not have at home at all. Filet mignon, turkey pies, stuffed chicken, so many fruits like apples and grapes and desserts, which, given my sweet tooth, was my favorite part. My cousins would be talking and playing outside, running around, and showing off their remote-controlled toys, and I would be stuffing my face with all kinds of food till I couldn't eat anymore. Then I would seat down in a corner and fall sleep till it was time to go home. Every now and then I'd go outside to play soccer if there was a good game happening but for the most part I was there to eat, and gosh did I eat? I wanted to gain weight and fill up a bit but to no avail. It was like I had an extra hole in my body, I could eat all I wanted and the next day on my walk to school I'd stop by at the pharmacy near my school to use their scale, I'd jump on it with hopes that I gained a few kilograms...nope, fuuuuuck my weight was unchanged. What do I have to do to have bigger legs, bigger arms, and to have an ass to fill up my saggy pants and those stupid clothes I wear at our family parties? I was flat as a pancake, and I used to wear two shorts under my pants to create the impression that I had some meat on my butt cheeks. I wanted my pants to fit me and not fall even when I had a belt on, I wanted to look better and not be talked about at parties...this shit was getting old and the fact that I didn't care anymore was not a good sign.

Needless to say, it wasn't very fun to go to family gatherings. To me everyone else had a better home, normal parents, decent cars, nice clothes, telephones with answer machines and long accordion cords, clean and comfortable shoes, nice toys, money for school snacks and plenty of food. I guess I had an inferiority complex, but I was inferior, period. I was extremely poor, not at all good looking like the rest of my cousins and my brother Cesar were. I had kinky afro hair, pimples all over my fucking face and body, bulgy eyes, buck teeth, long monkey arms, a terrible posture, a protruded chest which I was embarrassed to take my shirt off and people make fun of it, no ass, big stinky feet with fucked up shoes that belonged to my sister with my toes all cramped and my hills filled with blisters, funky and ugly clothes, 6' tall and 90lbs wet and did I mention I was so skinny that could walk on the rain and not get wet? I needed some positive words but that wasn't coming either... shit, life sucked at that junction.

So, I got my "no ass" a job. At thirteen years of age, I got a job at Legiao Brasileira de Assistencia, a non-profit organization which assisted the poor. Hell, it fit me perfectly I thought, I can get assistance there, if this organization can help the poor and needy, it sure as fuck can help me…I would fit right in.

"Damn it, if it wasn't enough to be poor, now I am going to work to help the poor people, like us?" I'd be saying to myself.

My mother's sister aunt Justina and uncle Joao Cordeiro ran the non-profit which was a government institution and they had hired my sister Moema as well and now I had a job as a typewriter. I went to a typewriting class five times a week for a month at this place near my Aunt Justina's house. I learned how to be the fastest and most efficient typewriter they ever had in that school, and I was on my way to change all the negativity surrounding me. Or was I? I was hungry in every sense of the word.

Goiania is a town of about 1.5 million people and surrounded by gigantic cattle farms, corn, soy, and rice fields, with agriculture making up for most of its economy. Every year at the end of June, there is a festival, a farmers market sort of festival which gathers farmers from all over the state and people from all over the country come to see the great looking animals, best produce in the country and listen to country music which is the heart and soul and the biggest export of the entire state of Goias, with the exception of soy. This festival is called "Pecuaria" (Livestock Festival) and it lasts for two weeks and it is where people go to be seen, to listen to country music, be entertain by rodeos and the bravest and craziest cowboys around the country, see famous musicians, people watch and hear the farmers talk about their crops, their cattle and their land and eat sugar glazed apples and some of the most delicious BBQ on the skewer one could find. The entire place smelled like food, and I don't remember ever having any money to eat anything there, but admission was free, and I love to go to see the latest pick-up trucks displayed for the well to do. To see what farmers were buying and to check out some of the finest women in the country. Goiania has a reputation for having seven beautiful women for each man and it is true, the secret I believe is in the cheese bread and all the fatty food they eat there, it makes the women mature young and my theory is that they look good now but won't be that hot in their later years because all that fat stuff will catch up to them. That was my way of rationalizing the fact that I had no chance of ever dating one of these gorgeous muses at Pecuaria but at least I knew that whoever dated them, the prospect of them looking that way in a few years was gloomy, and that made me feel less envious. I had a coach who used to say; "You show me a hot looking woman, I will show you a guy who's tired of having sex with her." That was so wrong I thought and I don't agree with him but I understood what he meant and it kind of made sense, and I am sure it is true for women as well, I think men and women get tired of each other more often than they admit.

My sisters and cousins and their friends love to go and meet boys, flirt with farmers, and get out of the house and the month of June is the only time the weather is cold enough to bring your winter clothing out of the closet in that part of the country. We didn't have any winter clothing but didn't' stop us from going and freezing our asses off to rub elbows with the well to do folks.

In one of these outings, we were walking from our house which wasn't too far from the venue where the livestock festival took place and there were my two sisters Moema and Tata, our cousins Helena and Leila and one of their friends Janete. Also, there were me and my brother Cesar who was about nine years old at the time. Cesar and I were walking in front of them, and I could hear them talking about boys, whispering, and laughing about who they were expecting to see at the festival. Suddenly, I could hear one of my cousins asking my sisters a question:

"What happened to Lenox? Look at him, he is so gawky, skinny, tall, strange looking and so different...what's with his ass?" Says Leila while everyone laughed out loud.

"Yes, what happened to Lenox? Cesar is soooo gorgeous with his blue eyes and curly blond hair, it's like they came from different parents?" Asked Helena rhetorically while laughing.

"Yes, Cesar is very cute and adorable and has always been but Lenox, well we don't know what happened to him." My sisters answered while giggling unapologetically.

I never forgot that day and couldn't believe how come they were so cruel to me? They probably thought I couldn't hear their conversation, but I did. Sure, I was used to that kind of abuse and was learning not to be upset anymore but it made me feel like I didn't belong there, I felt miserable, I felt not just poor, I felt like nobody really liked me or care to be nice to me, it seemed like it didn't matter where I went, I was always bullied and made fun of. I didn't need to hear that as often as I did, not from my sisters anyways but those comments were commonplace, and I was getting fucking tired of it.

I would go to the Livestock Festival and the entire time my only entertainment was to look at the food people were eating, envy the big pick-up trucks and dream about one day owning one myself and hopefully marry one of those dreamy girls with their beautiful skin, long and wavy hairs, and curvaceous bodies. In fact, my bucket list was very simple: A pick-up truck, a motorcycle and an apartment with a fridge filled with food and a long chord telephone with a fucking answer machine like those in the soap operas on TV. If I had that I would be happy because I knew the women would follow. I could be on my own then and never have to hear these motherfuckers treat me like I was a freak ever again.

My 13-year-old schedule was tight. I was going to school in the morning from 7:30 to noon, walked home for a quick lunch then walked about half mile to my job at LBA (Legiao Brasileira de Assistencia) from 1pm to 5pm Mondays to Fridays. I never missed a day of work, but I can't say the same about school. There were mornings when I'd venture out into the small forest two blocks away from my house where I would spend my mornings with a slingshot in my pocket, looking for birds and fruits while zoning out while observing the little monkeys who resided in those Jatoba trees - more popularly known as Stinking Toe trees. One of the largest trees in the Caribbean and South America, stinking toe can be found in a large brown pod, that somewhat resembles the shape of a toe. The fruit doesn't taste all that great, but the little monkeys love them, and I could spot them all over those beautiful trees. I was always intrigued and in awe of trees since a very young age.

At LBA I would spend my afternoons typewriting hundreds of documents for my aunt who was my boss at our department. I was a reliable good worker who never got distracted, I didn't talk to anyone, and I'd put my head down and got things done. I worked hard but I looked forward to having the daily thirty-minute breaks in between my afternoon shifts which allowed me to go outside and buy myself a treat occasionally; a juicy orange from Senhor Tito who had a small fruit cart in the parking lot. He had fruits, candies, chocolates, popcorn and pack of gums but the only one I could afford was an orange on Mondays when he would sell it to me for half the price. He'd peeled it off on a little machine that would go around the entire orange and take the skin off without a single brake on the peel. It was heaven for me to seat there and watch him do it. I'd eat every little piece of that sweet orange while all the other workers were taking a cigarette break and talking about their weekend at their farms or at the social clubs they belonged to.

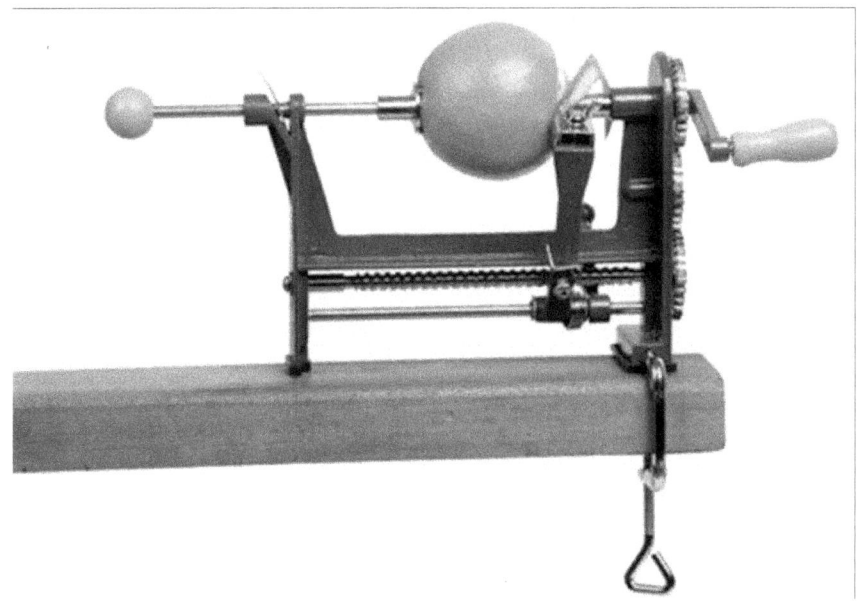

Orange Peeler

When you have an inferiority complex like I did for so long, you always think that everyone else has it better than you, no matter if that's true or not. My perception was my reality and to me, when people talked about their farms and all the fun they had during the weekend at this or that club, it would eat me inside and I wanted to have some of that as well. So, during my work break, I'd buy my half off orange and ask Senhor Tito for the unbroken peel which I'd tell him I could swing it around without breaking it. I'd bet with him that if I swung the peel around my head without breaking it for three, four or five full revolutions I'd get the following: three full revolutions and no break it meant I'd get a Honda CBR 450 motorcycle with paniers on the side so I could travel around the country with my beautiful imaginary girlfriend in the back. For four revolutions I'd earn a black four door Chevy-D20 Diesel pick-up truck with the plush stitched seats, and five revolutions was reserved for the big Kahuna prize; a two-bedroom apartment at a posh neighborhood with a fridge filled with good food and a telephone machine with a very long spiral cord so I could walk around my entire apartment while speaking on the phone with one of those gorgeous country girls I'd seen at the Pecuaria Fair.

"You crazy Lenox, it's not possible, the peel will break before you get to one full swing!" Senhor Tito murmured and laughed.

The orange peel would invariably break on the first or second go 'round but I didn't care because that routine would keep my hopes alive and all I wanted was to have hopes and dreams and the rest would take care of itself. I knew it was difficult and it had to be because the things I wanted were practically impossible and only achievable by the rich and famous in my 13-year-old inferiority complexed mind. My hope was renewed every Monday afternoon and I noticed how Senhor Tito was trying to help me by adjusting his peeling machine to make the orange peel thicker and stronger but to no avail, they'd always break on the first or second revolution. That routine was one of the best parts of my week till I was 17 years old when I stopped working at LBA and had a different goal in mind.

Every Monday afternoon I sat on that curb side next to Senhor Tito's cart and sucked on that juicy orange, once the juice was all gone, I would flip it inside out and eat the orange carpels on its entirety, leaving just the pith, the spongy white layer of the peel. Then I got up took my unbroken orange peel from his hand and try to rope those dreams over and over like a cowboy roping his prize calf from his horse. I knew that one day they'd come true.

"Why not me? I won't be like this my entire life. I won't be ugly, skinny, poor and hopeless my entire life." I unconsciously manifested not knowing what manifestation was.

I was on my way to great things I thought. I had a job which didn't pay much, but I could dream bigger now and I was feeling good. I started to be able to afford a small snack during school recess with the money I was making and all I needed now was to become a member of one of many social clubs so I could feel equal to those who brag about their weekends during their school or work breaks. In other words, I wanted to keep up with the joneses not at all knowing what that meant. As for the farm, I started with the hat, I bought a farmer's hat once and left it in my room so during my staring at the ceiling moments, that hat took me around a beautiful dream of one day owning a farm too, why not?

"Every farmer has a farmer's hat, and you can't own a farm without having a hat." I rationalized my splurging on a cheap farmers hat I found at the famers market in one of my trips there with my father.

In one of my walks to school, my walking buddy and friend Joao Carlos told me that this club called Club Ferreira Pacheco (SESI), had a soccer team and if we make the team, we could go practice every day there and, on the weekends, we could go jump in the pool and even eat some of the hot dogs they served on Sundays. He also said something that got my juices flowing.

"Lenox, I heard after practice they have very good snacks and sometimes full dinners and I hear people love it." Joao Carlos said with a smile on his face…the fucking guy knew what motivated me; food!

I convinced him to ride our bicycles to the registration office the next day and sign up for the soccer team. I was very hopeful and filled with joy because if I make the team, it will make my days and evenings completely full. I would not have to deal with the annoying piano lessons my sister Marina was teaching at home in the evenings, not to mention I'd get away from all the other shenanigans at my house.

We took it to the road on our bicycles the next day after my work shift to the Federacao Goiana de Futebol (Goiania Soccer Federation) and I was afraid they wouldn't take me because of my body type and the registration fee which might cost some money and I didn't have much to spare since I had splurged on my farm dream by purchasing the infamous farmer's hat.

"I may not be able to afford the registration depending how much it is." I told Joao Carlos with the hopes it wouldn't be much.

I didn't ask permission to my father either so, If I get in, I'd have to deal with all of that other dynamic in my house, but I was willing to do it because if I made the team, I'd be occupied from morning to night, and I would have great snacks, good food and new friends at the club, not to mention avoiding cleaning our bathroom on a daily basis.

"I HAVE TO GET IN, NO CHOICE!!!" I screamed to Joao Carlos with butterflies in my stomach and a huge smile on my face, as we rode our bicycles to the federation as if that was my ticket to freedom.

We parked and locked the bikes and took the long walk to the office which was located on the outside of the old Estadio Olimpico de Goiania (Goiania Olympic Stadium), please don't ask me why they called it "Olympic Stadium," it never was and never will be any Olympic games in that dump of a place, ever!!! We looked at the signs on the door, and when I saw "Federacao Goiana de Futebol," The butterflies were now flapping their wings in my stomach, and I wanted to give up right there and then. I asked Joao Carlos to speak, and I crossed my fingers on both hands for good luck and just asked God to please be kind, gentle and generous with me. We found the lady who was working behind an old cubicle and Joao Carlos told her that we wanted to sign up for the soccer team.

"We might be able to sign you up for soccer kid but not the bamboo stick standing next to you, he's way too tall and too skinny and we don't want him to get hurt. You boys should go next door to the Basketball Federation and sign him for that instead." Said the lady with a smirk on her face while looking me up and down.

We left that office in a hurry, and I was crushed, disappointed and feeling like God didn't give a rat's ass about me. We walked next door and Joao Carlos told me that we should sign up for basketball because he liked basketball too and he wanted to play with me. I thought it was the nicest gesture anyone had shown towards me ever, and I'd never forget it.

We signed up for basketball which held practices four times a week from 5:30pm to 7:30pm except on Thursdays. The only problem was that I've never played any organized basketball and I liked soccer better, my father was a soccer player, we could watch the soccer stars on TV during the world cup and I thought I was pretty good at it too.

What gave me hope however was that if we made the basketball team, we would receive a card with the club's membership which would give us the green light to come in anytime we wanted and play soccer just for fun in their beautiful fields, go in the three big swimming pools they had and the caveat: we could eat dinner and snacks with the basketball team every time we had practice. Wow, this was better than I dreamt of, and right there and then my life was forever changed. I shifted and was determined to make the team. Little did I know that I'd make the team regardless of my skills because I was very tall for a 13-year-old, and you can't teach height and length in basketball.

On Mondays, Tuesdays, Wednesdays and Fridays an old dark blue Ferreira Pacheco bus would pick us up from near Joao Carlos house on Vila Nova 5th avenue, and we would join a bunch of other kids who had been picked up on the way from the Olympic Stadium to the club on the south side of the city. On any given day there were 15 to 20 kids inside that bus. The first couple of weeks were fucking brutal. Every day when I stepped into the bus the other kids would laugh and say mean things about my skinny body and my hair. I was bullied constantly, but I had plenty of experience with that type of treatment already and learned not to care as much and decided that if I don't show any reaction to their jokes, they'd soon find someone else to pick on. Eventually they got to know me, and the jokes subsided to a manageable level.

I was actually surprised by how little I felt hurt with the mean jokes and I guess all the years of being poked fun at by my own family prepared me for that new experience and I was getting desensitized by that non sense.

I didn't really know how to play basketball that well. I had a cousin named Adriano who played with me in front of my house and some pick-up ball at the Club Jao every now and then when he would bring me along to play with him. We'd get competitive amongst ourselves, and he'd beat me most of the time. I wasn't selected often to play on the full court pick-up games, but I enjoyed watching and learning. This new gig was a different and higher level for sure, guys were taller and stronger, but that never intimidated me, except for some for their skill set and the ability to jump which I thought it was fascinating.

At Ferreira Pacheco I was exceling, learning, growing and being fed well four times a week and sometimes on weekends when we had a scrimmage or a game with another friendly team. Little did I know that our coach had plans to sign us up to compete in the state's tournament in the following year. I was 13-years-old and by then about 6'3" and a solid 95 pounds wet and loaded. I took basketball as my refuge, my escape from school and work and especially from home. My days were full: I leave home at 7:00 am, go to school, come home, eat lunch and go to work from 1:30 to 5:00, track all the way home, change and go to basketball practice from 5:30 to 7:30pm, shower and ate at the club and by the time I got home I'd be bushed and completely tired for my homework which I still had to get it done. School was taking a backseat to work and basketball and all my incessant daydreaming. The busier I became the more I enjoyed it. My life was starting to change, and I could see that I was going to take it to basketball, and it became everything to me. I literally walk, ate and slept basketball and competition and while staring at the ceiling which had clear images now, an imaginary movie would play on the white canvas of our bedroom ceiling and it wasn't blank anymore and not even in black and white...it had colors and shapes and I loved it, I was hooked.

In one of those weekends when everyone was gone from the house, I hung an old garbage can on top of the tree in front of our house and made a hole in the bottom of it, put some strings my sisters use to make hangers with on the edges to mimic a net, demarcated and made a single court on the asphalt with old chalk I'd bring from school and, BANM!!! I had my private court and could play anytime I wanted now. I'd play with my brother Cesar, my cousin Adriano, my friend Joao Carlos, but most of all, I played by myself. I shot free throws, I did reverse layups, I learned how to use my left hand, how to play on the post, how to use angles, how to shoot and rebound because my basket on the tree didn't have a backboard. It was just the bottomless garbage can nailed to one of the branches of the tree, so I had to learn how the ball would bounce when I missed a shot and had to rebound without the ball hitting the ground first because cars drove fast on that corner and it was a blind spot and we couldn't see them coming. Sometimes they were so close that I had to be fast and agile to jump out of the way while the drivers screamed at me in anger.

"Get the fuck out of the road before you get killed you skinny bum." That was the daily chorus as drivers yelled from their cars.

I realize very soon that it was better and easier to just not miss my shots and take good ones and make them, than to shoot from anywhere and run after the rebounds because if I'd miss my shot, I was roadkill to all the noisy muffler less cars coming around the corner.

That was good training and to this day I believe the best players have great instincts and there's no better way to develop good instincts than to play the way I was playing.

At Ferreira Pacheco, the coach Roberto Bolinha was taken a liking to my style and the way I played. He would reference me to the other players and ask me to show them how to do a certain move or demonstrate a drill and I felt important. He would ask me to show my teammates how to block out during rebounding, how to pivot my foot and head and ball fake, how to guard the opposing player by staying in front of them but pushing them to use their weaker hand or denying the opposing player the ball all together in the wings. I could see the game different than my teammates and my anticipation on defense was better than most. In practices and games, I'd get a good number of steals, most rebounds, most blocks and cause the opposing team turnovers often, simply by anticipation and being ahead with my thought process. I credit all those skills to playing on the hung garbage can, being aware of the cars, the bounce of the rebound and having no backboard to read the direction of the ball when I missed a shot. No coach can teach you that.

I don't think I was a great scorer even though I scored lots of points often. But I score lots of points on offense rebounds, free throws, steals, and those so called, and how fitting when I think about it now; "garbage points."

I couldn't shoot the ball very well. Perhaps my body was in constant growth mode, and it took me years to become a decent shooter. At first, every shot I took was a backboard shot. I guess because I never had a backboard at my basket on the tree at home, when I started to play with the backboard, I found it very easy to use that big square to get the ball thru the hoop. It didn't matter where I shot from, I'd always use the backboard…so, the coaches didn't want me to shoot much because most players never really used the backboard, especially when shooting from the top of the key.

Where I really excelled was on defense though. I loved playing against taller and stronger guys. For some unknown reason, I could guard both the tallest and strongest and the shortest and fastest guys on the opposing team. I could help on defense and make life easier for my teammates and very difficult for the opposing team with my longer than normal arms. I got so good that I was asked to join a State team to play a national tournament in Brasilia, 200 miles away from Goiania in my first year of playing organized ball.

Wow, my name was on the newspapers for the first time, and I was amongst the best players in my state and one of the 12 players to represent the state in a national tournament. Never thought this would happen, NEVER!!! These kids were good players and just a year ago I used to watch them and be in awe of their skills and now I am traveling with them in the same bus and sharing the dormitories made from an old school classroom, eating with them and playing with them…a dream come thru!

We took 3rd place in the tournament out of 20 teams. I started on the bench for the first game but became a started on the second and never came from the bench again after that. When I came home from that tournament everyone started to respect me, older and - in my mind - famous players wanted to be my friends and would invite me to their workouts/practices and their pickup games. I knew then that I had found my passion for the rest of my life, basketball, competition, sports. It gave me the confidence I needed, and my height was now an asset rather than a liability or a reason for jokes. Well, people still fucked with me often but now I had more important dreams to dream.

I played volleyball, soccer, ping pong, I swam, I played at home and every weekend from morning to night till the lights were turned off and my feet were bleeding already. I wouldn't eat anything after breakfast all day on Saturdays and Sundays till I came home in the evening. My pickup game teams would play all day and rarely lose a game, mainly because of my play and how much better I made the other players play. I was addicted to basketball and hooked on competition and winning. I would watch everything and anyone with a ball in their hands or on their feet. I would watch Formula 1 racing for the fast cars and beautiful women but also watch every sport and have all the pictures of best players, best racing drivers, famous sports celebrities and know their stories, their families, and their path to glory. Sports was my life and still is to this day.

CHAPTER IX
Like a Feather

I n the following year I was on a fast track and became a reliable player under the system of full court pressure our coach had implemented, and we won the State championship against the best team in the State of Goias; Joquei Clube de Goias and coached by a famous national team super star and Olympic athlete Adilson Nascimento. Nobody thought it was possible to beat the loaded with talent and resources Joquei Clube. They had dominated basketball in our city and state for many years and had the best resources, money to pay the players, scholarships to offer, expensive and well-known coaches and they were in downtown, with beautiful facilities, a physio room, trainers, swimming pools, weight room and a sauna which to this day I still can smell the aroma of pine and cedar coming from the steam room. To me those perks were something that I could only dream of when I watched TV and they'd show the lives of the rich and famous sports stars…definitely not for me I thought.

I wasn't the best player on my team, but maybe the glue that kept the team together with my play and defense. I was a passionate player for sure, tall, skinny, and becoming more athletic every day, hard worker and smart, a great teammate, reliable and a fighter. After winning the State championships, I was again amongst the best 12 players to represent the State in a national championship and travel out of state to play a national tournament once again, this time in Sao Paulo, a 20 million people city and a mecca of basketball and sports in Brazil. I saw my name in the newspaper by accident amongst the other 12 kids (9 of the other players came from Joquei Clube and two from Ajax Club and only me from

SESI) and I didn't really understand why my name was there, I wasn't really believing that I was selected again.

I showed up to practice with the State team in good form and I knew everyone there was older, more experienced, and better than me on paper and more confident than I was and most important, they had great sneakers and high socks with two or three horizontal stripes on them while I was still wearing my father's working black socks and my sister's Congas. So, I did the only thing I could do, I played and worked harder than anyone else. I arrived early and stayed late after practice and work on everything and every weakness I had from ball handling, passing, shooting, defense schemes to jumping drills, and played one on one and two on two with every single person who wanted to play, weather they were basketball players or not.

During one of the tune-up games we had, I had no hopes that the coach was going to put me in but one of the players got hurt and we needed someone to play defense on this other kid who was having a field day against us.

"How do you feel Lenox, do you think you can stop that kid from scoring on us?"

Coach Celio from Ajax asked me during timeout.

"I feel great coach, I feel like a feather, I can fly, and yes, I can stop him."

I replied without any hesitation, but I was literately shitting in my pants with so much fear because this was high stakes, this was the big leagues.

"Don't fuck up Lenox, don't you fuck it up." The little annoying voice kept on whispering in my ears.

Everyone started laughing in the huddle because even though they knew what I meant, they thought it was ridiculous what I said since I was a newcomer and people didn't take me seriously. They also joke around with my appearance at times and called me all kinds of names like spaghetti, Q-tip and everything else in between. That stuff was getting old, and it made me depressed sometimes and sad that my own teammates were cruel to me and made fun of my appearance. But in hindsight, it was also what gave me the motivation to work harder and the desire to leave Goiania one day and never come back again. Well, now I just gave these motherfuckers more material to pick on me with the "feeling like a feather" line and I had to deal with it for a long time. I went out there wearing a state jersey and I played well, represented my state and my family with honor but I knew I wasn't going to get many opportunities to score or get plenty of minutes, so I committed myself to shadow that kid on the other side and not let him catch the ball, even if I have to commit 5 fouls in 5 minutes, I was going to make my presence felt and I did. The kid got frustrated and pushed me around couple of times, called me "toothpick" and a bunch of other names but I didn't care and didn't let him get to my head. I was committed to not let him to touch the ball for as long as I was on the court…

"I will follow and shadow this motherfucker, even if he goes to the bathroom." That was my attitude and I even managed to get couple of steals and scored couple of baskets besides the two free throws I earned from being pushed around by him. We won that game and the coach praised and showered me with lots of compliments and that's all I needed; for the first time in my life, I felt like a confident kid, and I hang on to that feeling to this day. Anytime things get difficult and challenging for me in life, I reach back on that well and I find the courage and remind me of the "like a feather" feeling to manage a favorable outcome, it works every time. It is a state of mind for sure.

I made my reputation in that one opportunity I got and from that day on I started in every game in my club team and with the state teams which I was getting used to be called to and be the defense anchor. I was given the toughest guy on the opponent's team to guard, and I loved it. It didn't matter if the opponent best player was a guard or a post, I could guard anyone and the better they were the more motivated I got. I wouldn't score a lot of points but that never was my thing anyways, I was just happy to belong somewhere, and I felt I was finding my passion in life. Perhaps that's the reason that later in life I loved Dennis Rodman (Detroit Pistons, San Antonio Spurs, Chicago Bulls) and never minded his off the court antics. Like me I thought he was misunderstood and had something to prove all the time. I didn't have Rodman's off court antics, but I could relate to his style and boldness.

I wanted to practice all the time and I could play all day if I didn't have to go to school, work or go home. My name was appearing on the newspapers sports page quite often and I was earning the respect of older players who were playing in the adult division. I would be called up to practice with the super stars, guys that were playing with the Brazilian National team, competing in Olympic games and international competition all over the world. I couldn't even sleep sometimes because I was afraid this whole thing was a dream, and I was going to wake up from it any time and my life was going to go back to what it was before basketball; staring at the ceiling above my bunk bed in search for a way out of whatever I was going thru. In hindside, I think all that staring at the ceiling was unconscious meditation and some sort of manifestation of a better life.

I worked very hard, school became a chore to me because with the little spare time I had between school, work and basketball, I just wanted to get my work done and go to practice. My life was busy and when I got home, I was so hungry that I would eat anything my father would bring to me. Usually, it was soup with a fried egg on top which was once limited to my father only but now that gorgeous sunny side up egg was making into my late night menu as my father started to see my progress. The soup was usually the leftovers from past meals because nothing would go to waste in my house, we couldn't afford that. I loved the nightly soups and the fried egg, and I still love it to this day. I liked my busy schedule, it kept me out of the house and out of trouble even though my grades were dropping a bit and I started to falter in math.

As the school year got to an end, I was given a chance to make up my math grade if I was going to move on to 8th grade, but to no avail, I couldn't pass the class and had to repeat 7th grade on its entirety because I couldn't pass my math finals and my overall scores weren't enough to carry me to the 8th grade. I tried to go to summer school and pick up some extra work and bring my math grades up, but I was too involved with basketball and too discouraged and lacking motivation to do schoolwork with so many exciting things happening on the other side of my life. I was also discovering girls and growing even more conscious about my skinny body and long arms and legs not to mention masturbation which by then was starting to make a daily appearance in my already busy life. By the end of December, right before Christmas, I knew I had failed math after summer school (summer in the south hemisphere is the opposite than the northern hemisphere) and I would have to repeat the entire year and all the classes I had taken on 7th grade. All my friends would be moving on to the next grade and I would be staying in the same classroom with new classmates, and completely embarrassed for having to repeat the entire year all over again. Can life get any more difficult and more embarrassing? I learned a valuable lesson about balancing all my activities and finding a common ground between school, sports, family, work and growing up with so little guidance and nurturing.

The biggest challenge about failing school was that I had to go home and tell my family about it and my father was probably going to literally twist my neck, hang me upside down on the guava tree and watch me struggle to slow death, just like the way he did with those chickens every Sunday. My only hope was that he wouldn't dunk me in boiling water and burn my feet afterwards…hopefully anyways!

On my walk home after the last day of summer school, I had an eureka moment and decided that I wasn't going to tell anyone I failed 7th grade. I felt I was so insignificant to everyone at home that they wouldn't even know what grade I was, and I am the only one who goes to that school anyways, and my family were so busy with their own shit that nobody would even find out. It made perfect sense to me: If they asked me, I would tell them I passed with flying colors, and nobody would never know I was repeating 7th grade, how could they? I signed my stepmother's name on all my report cards the entire year anyways and nobody asked me about it. It's not like in the USA, where parents are involved and helicoptering and hovering over their kids' lives. In my household, nobody ever came to watch one of my games, nobody really checked my report cards or bother to ask me if I needed help with my homework, if I needed anything, if I was sad nobody asked my why, if I was happy no one got too excited about it either, if I was depressed, who the fuck cares? There was a big disconnect with all the needs a child becoming a teenager had but there were just too many of us and everyone was just fighting their own demons, carrying their own weight, and carving their own space in life thru the surviving mode.

So, I thought all I needed was to continue my own path going forward and I didn't think anybody even knew what grade I was on anyways till I'd be old enough to move out and be on my own. If they ask,

I can always answer whatever I want and they'd believe me, I thought… naively!!!

That was the longest walk of my life though. That journey from school to home that day is one of those days in my life which I will never forget: It was raining hard and there were thunderstorms, the air was heavy, and the sky was dark gray with lots of lightning strikes which is common in Goiania. I decided to enjoy the rain instead of hiding from it, and let it sort of cleanse me, wash all my troubles away with hopes that if I was lucky enough, I'd get hit by one of those scary lightnings and its scary thunderous collisions putting an end to my meager and insignificant existence once and for all…solving my predicament all at once…deep inside I was scared and fucking confused about everything.

At last, I would change the narrative of the joke that I could walk on rain and not get wet…fuck off, I not only can get wet, but I also can get hit by lightning, take that you ass holes! I was in a state of fuck everyone and everything, why can I get a break when things are starting to go so well for me? Why didn't I pass the stupid math class and useless algebra bullshit which I will never use it again in my life? WHY can't I ever get a fucking break?

I had decided I didn't care what my dad did to me if I were to make it home and tell the truth, I surrendered to my fear and the prospects of my destiny and whatever happens after that. I would just be a participant in the process but not suffer any longer. However, If I keep my mouth shut and don't try to talk too much, I'd be all right. Nobody will find out anyways, why and how would they unless I tell them?

"Hit me lightning, I am right here, why don't you fucking strike me at once and put an end to this?" I screamed in the middle of that crazy rainstorm while sobbing like a hungry child that I was, soaking wet from rain and tears and terrified with the prospect of having to face my father, let alone the embarrassment of repeating 7th grade all over again.

I walked into our living room all wet from the torrential rain I had showered in, and my dad, surprisingly and unusually early from work was seating on the old checkers black and red rocking chair he had been gifted by auntie Cro. I didn't say much and went straight to the bathroom looking for a towel to dry myself off. I come out of the bathroom with the towel already soaking wet.

"How come you are wet Lenox?" Asked my father with a suspicious voice.

"It's raining outside the entire afternoon, and I was hungry. So, I decided not to wait for the rain to pass." I replied with confidence and without hesitation but thinking "what a stupid question because it's raining like a motherfucker outside. Can't you see the fucking rain man?" I thought irritated out of pure fear and terrified of what might happen if he found out the truth.

"How's school, done yet for this year?" Asked my father which sounded very fishy to me. I found the timing of his question almost too obvious, just like the why I was wet question a second earlier because I knew I had flanked math and will have to repeat 7th grade but he never asked about my grades or school...ever!!! I was thinking what kind of question is this? What does he know and why is he interested now? Jesus fucking Christ!!!

"Where is your report card, can I see it Lenox?" Asked my father following up his first question without a chance for me to answer it.

"Shit, what is this now? He never asked me any of these questions ever before, nobody had, why now? How do I tell him that I have been signing my report cards with my stepmom's signature? How do I tell him I have failed 7th grade and will have to repeat it?" I am in a heated dialogue with a bunch of other voices in my head as confusion settles in.

"I don't have the report card yet, summer school is still in session." I replied

My dad had a suspicious look on his face but at this point I am thinking everything is suspicious because I am lying, and a lying guilty mind works in complicated ways.

"He could be bluffing; he doesn't know anything. I just have a guilty mind so stick to your story Lenox, stick to your fucking story!" My thoughts were discombobulated.

His deep blue eyes were bulging out of the eye sockets again, and I thought he knew what was going on and my jig was up. He let me get deeper into my story just to see how far I could take it.

"I guess you are going to go back on the rain and walk with me to your school to get your report card, just me and you." With a tone of sarcasm in his voice.

I thought he was fishing for information, and I wasn't about to volunteer anything to him. It was raining cats and dogs outside and I knew my dad wouldn't put a foot outside the house under that kind of weather and I wanted to gain time to perhaps run away for good next morning and never come back, thinking that was my chance once and for all. Besides my dad was so busy with so much on his mind that he'd forget very important things often and maybe if I hold him off for today, he'd forget about this school shit and about me too the next day.

"Sure, it's really wet outside dad, but summer school isn't over yet and the report cards aren't out yet but if you want to go…let's go! I am curious about my report card too." I said that calling on his bluff and keeping to my story since he never ever went to school with me and he wasn't about to go out now on the rain, lightning and thunderstorms, no fucking way…right? Wrong!

He was seating on the checkered rocking chair with his black socks still on as if he's just got home too. It was unusual for my father to be home that early, but it was a stormy day and taxi drivers don't like to drive during heavy rain and lightning storms like that. Goiania gets flooded with the lightest of rain falls and the streets turn into rivers, damaging their taxis with all that sludge. He put on his impeccably clean and shiny black fake leather shoes he bought at the Vila Nova farmers market stand across from serial killer Antonio's barber shop and calmly stood up in an eerie and methodical way.

"This ain't my father, he's not methodical and calm like this," I was thinking. It was like I went "all in" with a seven and a deuce in high stakes poker and trying not to give away anything, hoping and praying he didn't call me with a pair of aces.

We took it to the wet streets towards my school and the rain had now subsided a bit but still wet and loud with all the thundering and lightning. The sky cleared up a bit and the fresh smell of wet plants and wet dirt was in the air. I have always loved that smell of nature, and especially of red dirt after the rain. I was sweating profusely but Goiania is a very humid place and when it rains hard and the sun picks out like it that, you can see the paved roads steaming like a fucking sauna.

About three blocks away, I noticed that my father was calm and collected and that was unusual for this brute and impatient man…oh gosh, his eerie silence was another challenge, he wouldn't say anything to me and it felt like those three blocks and however few minutes walking felt like hours and not good news for me because he was never calm and collected and that whole scene looked and felt awkward. My guilty mind was racing, my heart palpitating out of my chest and perhaps there was a chance he was fucking with me because he didn't know anything, right? How could he? I was floundering and faltering, and the guilty mind was weakening slowly, he was mining me without having to do anything and I fell for it.

"He must know something because in fourteen years he never came even close to my school and I doubt he even know the address and now, he's walking to school with me on the fucking rain? Fuck this shit, he's got the pair of aces and he's calling my seven/deuce all in bluff." I thought while the voices were screaming in my ears louder and louder.

We walked side to side without exchanging a single word for about three blocks. I was completely drenched with sweat because by then the rain had completely stopped and all I could see was the steam from the asphalt fogging my vision and my thoughts. When we got passed couple blocks after Radio Brasil Central, an old building which housed one of the oldest AM radio stations in our city, I gave in and folded my cards.

"I didn't pass my math class and I flunked summer school and I will have to repeat the entire 7th grade next year." I fessed up while looking straight at him and scared shitless of his deep, bright blue eyes now, calmly, and intensely staring at me without a single blink.

"Run back home and get a skinny guava tree branch from the backyard, take the leaves off and wait for me in the back near the water spigot where I sharpen my knives, I will be there shortly." My father was detailed with his instructions and spoke without any hesitation. His eerie and calm demeanor was the scariest thing I have ever faced up to that point. It was surprising because he didn't shout like he used to. "This shit's going to get crazy." That was my biggest fear that he would hurt me badly as I had seen it doing to my sisters.

We were across the street from this little bar near the Radio Brasil Central building where my father stopped by daily to get a shot of his favorite cachaça and a piece of crispy pig skin (torresmo) which he took a bite on after his swig on the high alcohol content fear destroyer "gole de pinga" (shot of hard liquor).

"Go home Lenox, go home and wait for me." He shouted as he crossed the street to his favorite bar. I headed home, I knew I was doomed.

Many thoughts came to mind on that short walk home but the clearest and one that made most sense to me was to just keep walking and never look back, what else do I have to lose?

"Perhaps this was the moment I have been waiting for all my life, the excuse I needed to run away and it's now right here in front of me. Just disappear and never come back Lenox, just go away and he won't be able to touch you or hurt you...run Lenox, just fucking run!!!" One of the voices was now screaming in my head and it made so much sense to me.

Suddenly, for some reason unbeknownst to me, I had a huge sense of relief because when he said guava tree, I figured he was going to ask me to get a rope too and tie my feet up, hang me on that tree, twist my neck and hang me upside down like the chickens on Sunday. As dramatic as it may sound, I was ready for my death ceremony. At least I knew how I was going to die, and I made peace with it.

"This is for the best and there won't be any more suffering and embarrassments. No more feeling skinny or hideous or whatever else it made me feel inferior...fuck you all." Besides, without me there will be one less kid to feed and worry about, there will be more food and everything else for my siblings after I struggled while hanging upside down on that guava tree branch with a broken neck just waiting for the boiling water dunk.

I felt like death has come upon me and I was ready for it, besides basketball, my life sucked anyways, and I was ready for whatever my father did to me. I did exactly that, despite resisting the temptation or just keep on walking into a road to nowhere and never returning again; I ran home from where we were, went to the guava tree, cut a long and skinny branch, took all the leaves off and waited for my torturer to arrive. I had made a deal with one of the voices in my head that I wasn't going to cry, not make a scene, and cause no drama, whatever he does to me, I was going to take it and surrender to the punishment because I deserved it and hopefully it will be quick and if he kills me I would even thank him for it, if I bleed, don't look at it (which I knew I would bleed because I had seen my sisters get spanked and beaten before). However, the other less dramatic voice in my head was getting louder and demanding my attention.

"Let him do his thing and if he doesn't kill you, it is going to hurt and probably bleed badly, and you will be bruised and not able to go to practice for a few weeks, but this too will pass and it's only fair I get punished for signing my report cards all year long and for failing 7th grade so disgracefully. Take the punishment and don't complain about it but you will live." This other stubborn voice would reason on the other side of my head while the more dramatic one would say the opposite and there was a battle of many difference voices going on all at once with me in the middle trying to reason an unreasonable predicament.

My dad walked into the house, and nobody said a word. All my sisters and my stepmom Nida were there but nobody dared to take my side. How could they? I was in the backyard next to the spigot which he kept a lime rock under where he sharpened his knives. I don't recall seeing my sisters and my stepmom seating there when I walked thru the house and how long it took from the time that I ran home from where we were and when he finally met me outside but I could hear his steps, the noise of the rusted and bent front gate, the opening of the door that would get stuck on the bottom from the humidity of the rain and the wood expanding. I could see it in my thoughts and I wish I was laying in my bunkbed while staring at my blank canvas on the ceiling; my sisters desperate faces in the living room couch and what they must be thinking about. I could only imagine how they felt the many times he did the same to them. Are they going to stop him perhaps? Is someone going to say anything at all? His steps were getting louder and stronger and without a single word, he came to where I was, I could smell the alcohol and the pig skin on his breath and that was one of the few moments I saw my mother's image in front of me...How much I wanted my mother there to protect me from that man was something I couldn't even explain, even if I tried. He took the guava branch I left on top of the limestone and without a word he grabbed my left arm and with one swift move lifted me up from the ground and whooped me and whooped me again and again and again till my legs were cut and bleeding, my skin bruised and the cuts getting deep into my flesh. He wouldn't stop and the more he hit me, the less I wanted to cry and the less I cry the more he hit me, like he hated me and wanted to see me suffer instead of just killing me and getting me out of my misery. For the first time in my life, I didn't have any feelings, no hatred, no despair, no fear, and a complete surrendering to a no pain state of mind which was disturbing to me because I was used to feeling pain, albeit physically, mentally, emotionally, or otherwise.

It felt like that moment lasted forever, and I didn't think I was going to make it, I didn't believe in love than, and I knew this would end badly because if I don't cry, he's not going to stop, he was raging with anger and hatred. If I cry, he will think I am weak so I stuck to my plan, and I never reacted to that beating. I just stood there, all 6'3" and 95lb of skin and bone soaking wet from rain, fear, sweat and blood and I took my father's abuse, his rage, his anger, and his frustrations and disappointments with the world and now with me. Come to think of it, he was disappointed at his own life, at his own failures or lack of opportunities, his memories of his beatings by his older brother and his anger about how the fuck he's got all these young kids and what happened to his life…Those must've had been what his feelings were about because nothing else made any sense to me. How can you hurt your kid like that?

When he was done, I sat not too far from the crime scene, on this cold concrete sidewalk next to the spigot and limestone, I saw splashes of blood everywhere on the walls and cement and I opened the water faucet and I sat on the limestone, put my legs under the faucet and let the cold water run on my bruised and cut legs and body. I felt the burn and the skin cringing with the burning and pain, but I didn't cry, I didn't react or felt anything, It was like I had died and now this was life in hell.

"How can I continue to live in this hell of a place after this? How?" All the voices in my head were now in clear harmony and I felt like I was levitating, I felt like a feather again but this time I was floating for real.

Then I realized that my father was teaching me a lesson the way he knew how, the way he was taught his lessons when he was a kid. It didn't make it right obviously but that's what he knew. The whooping however was one thing but there was the other elephant in the room.

"How am I going to face everyone else and how can I forgive my dad for hurting me so badly physically but even more mentally and emotionally, how?" I pondered about that often my entire adolescence and for a great part of my young adult life.

Truth is, although nothing justified that type of punishment, he didn't know any better, he didn't have the skill set or the tools in his toolbox (so to speak) to deal with me and his family. He didn't have any emotional intelligence to recognize that the beating and the medicine he was applying on us was worse than the disease, but he was never talked to, loved, or nurtured himself as a child.

The other side of my brain was in conflict because all my friends were moving on to 8th grade except for me. On top of that, my legs, body, and ego were still bruised, bleeding and hurting, but my resolve and strength were tested. I felt nothing except confusion towards my father who never took a minute to help me with math, or with any homework. But how could he? He didn't know fucking algebra himself...who does?

For a while I felt hatred towards him for beating us kids and especially my sisters. I felt resentment for never once driving me to school or help me with math and never showing up to watch me play or practice, but how could he? He didn't know that kind of math, he didn't have the time to drive me and all my sisters and brothers to school, he didn't have the time to watch my practices or my games, he had to work to put whatever little food we had on the table and a roof over our heads. I hang my hat on his qualities instead of his shortfalls and that got me thru it, that made me understand that kids are precious, kids grow to be adults one day and have children of their own. I also learnt and understood that parents bring their history and baggage with them, and I was lucky to still have a father who cared enough to straighten my skinny ass up and teach me thru the only way he knew how, violence, physical and emotional abuse. Obviously, I'd rather my father talked and reasoned with me in a way I could understand and comprehend. I'd prefer he showed me how I was going on the wrong path by failing school but that wasn't my path or his, that wasn't our relationship dynamic. I chose to accept that at least he cared enough to ridicule himself with the hopes I didn't turn out like him; an abusive father, a broken man who couldn't find his way out of low paying jobs and womanizing habits. I accepted that not everyone has the skills to raise children and my father wasn't an exception.

Truth be told, I had plenty of resentment towards my father for so many reasons, but I learned to let them all go, to accept that he only knew what he learned and what he learned he had to apply to eight kids, and a second wife after my mother died. It must've been brutal for my old man to accept his underpaid and overworked jobs as mechanic and cab driver and probably robbed him of any ambition he might've had and took all his time, even on weekends.

I suffered and so did my siblings and our moms but how could we continue to resent him given his circumstances? I guess I could, anyone could, and some do forever, but those questions engulfed my thoughts and it pushed me forward, forced me to keep starring at the ceiling in complete silence for hours on end and gave me perspective and empathy for my father's deep troubling behaviors.

"What's wrong with this man? Why is he so unhappy and so difficult to live with? Why can't he just love me and talk to me?" My curious mind and my questions were incessant and there weren't any answers coming from anywhere because we were all questioning the same thing, but nobody had answers or knew how to deal with it.

I guess when you are a kid, you don't understand things and the world revolves around you and your questions. After that whooping, I couldn't go anywhere for couple of months because my legs were bruised and scabbing still, and I was too embarrassed to let anyone see it and too ashamed and embarrassed to have to lie or explain it. My father and I didn't speak for a few months, and I couldn't understand how someone could hurt his child that much. Sure, my transgressions needed to have consequences but the whooping drew much more than just blood…it drew hatred, confusion and a broken heart.

At that time in my life as a fourteen-years-old kid just going thru puberty with so much drama and trauma under my belt. That beating drew my wrath towards my father, my sisters, who didn't do anything to stop him, my stepmom who sometimes I felt didn't have a backbone on her spine, that damned city of Goiania which never felt like home, I never belonged there or in that house. My days were counted and since that afternoon I started to make plans about when and how I was going to leave and never come back again.

CHAPTER X
If It Ain't Broke, Break It!

That summer I was as lost as a "cachorro em dia de mudanca" (a dog in a moving day), as lost as a person can be. I barely did anything fun outside with my friends. I wasn't speaking with anyone about anything, and I spent most of my time when I was at home staring at the ceiling from my bunk bed. I would listen to music on the sound system I had purchased and financed at a C&A department store in 48 monthly small installments and paying from my job earnings and my first purchase ever with my own money. Listening to music was my refuge. Milton Nascimento, Caetano Veloso, Talking Heads, James Taylor, Carly Simon, The Beatles, those were my intimate new friends, with them I traveled around the world and imagined all the places I wanted to visit, the people I wanted to meet, the food I wanted to eat, the cars and motorcycles I wanted to own, the teams I wanted to play for, the girls I wanted to date, the shoes I wanted to wear, the high socks with two or three stripes I wanted to possess that would hide my scars, the muscles I craved would eventually grow in my body, the hair I desired to have… with their music I found courage to keep dreaming and the strength to deal with everything and anything thrown my way.

When the school year came around again, that's when I realized how badly I fucked up by failing and having to repeat 7th grade. When I saw my classroom and classmates, I became depressed, embarrassed, and again so lost!!! All the same classes, the same teachers, the same smells except I had brand new classmates who never ceased to ask me how come I was repeating the year again. Eventually that feeling of desperation, the feeling of wanting to disappear and run away to an unknown corner of someplace where nobody would know who I was and didn't have to explain so much of my story, eventually those feelings subsided, and I settled in my new/old world in 7th grade...again!

During recess, I would hang out with my old friends now in 8th grade and I dove into math. I got so good at it that one particular day at the end of the first semester in June, right around halfway thru the school year, our overconfident math teacher Mr. Santos got really brave and gave us a very difficult equation challenge and he vowed to give anyone who was the first to get the correct answer the highest grade midway through the school year and the prize was that the winner wouldn't have to attend his math classes again for the rest of the year, which meant; from August thru December the winner would be free from going to math classes. He gave us 20 minutes to figure out the equation and we needed to present the answer to him in front of the entire class and explain how we got to it. I wanted that prize so bad that I was the first one to turn in what I thought was the right answer for the assignment except that I didn't have it right. Couple of other students brought their equation sheet to Mr. Santos who was seating behind an old wooden desk in the middle of classroom, but theirs too were incorrect. I kept looking at the clock on the wall behind Mr. Santos desk and hearing the tik-tok noise in my head. I racked my brain and was certain that I was on the right track with my calculations, so I simply added a zero to my original final answer and took it back to Mr. Santos and, to my surprise he rang this little yellow and broken on one side bell he carried with him when he wanted to get everyone's attention.

"We have a winner; Lenox has the correct answer!" Mr. Santos announced to the class with a surprised look on his face.

"Wow, what the fuck...seriously?" I couldn't believe it. We were in June and the school year in Brazil starts in February, right after the Carnival celebration.

By getting this answer right in June I had already passed my math class and I didn't have to attend Mr. Santos classes anymore for the next 6 months. I felt like a winner for sure and it is debatable to think that my father had anything to do with that. That his whooping caused me to dive into math like that, but the sweat, steam, pain, blood, embarrassment and suffering of that stormy day no longer hurts but it triggers sensations and thoughts which I decided to turn into a positive experience instead of one of self-pity, hatred, or resentment. I love my father and I admire him for sticking with us, for how much work he had to do and how he provided and never gave us away to the other uncles and aunties who offered to raise us when I would completely understand if he had succumbed to the temptation of getting help raising his kids after my mother died and again when we came back from the Amazon. He didn't and I am thankful for it.

So, during math classes which I was now excused from attending for the rest of the year, I would go to the playground and play basketball with some of the older kids who had a different recess time and were always playing basketball. It felt so liberating and such a blessing at the right time in my life to have won something. Everyone thought I was cutting classes to play basketball but I didn't care, I wasn't.

When I told my family that I had passed my math class already in June, they didn't believe me either, how can I blame them? But this time I had the pair of aces in my hand, and I didn't have to bluff or fold.

7th grade was a breeze the second time around and the following year I was offered to have my school paid for via a scholarship to study at Colegio Objetivo, which was the school for the rich kids in my city. In exchange for the scholarship, I had to take my basketball talents to archrival Joquei Clube de Goias. That was a difficult decision for me because I loved SESI and the Ferreira Pacheco Club. I loved my coach and my teammates; I enjoyed the bus rides and the joking around in our daily 30 minutes ride from Vila Nova to SESI and most of all, I was being fed after practice with good and plentiful nutritious food.

I knew I had to accept the scholarship because I was the only one of the eight siblings in my family who'd have an opportunity to study at such a prestigious private school designed for the rich and famous in my town. I wanted to stay at SESI because people were no longer making fun of my appearance or my father's black working socks I'd be wearing, or joking about the hole on my sister's white Conga shoes I was sporting daily. Besides, I had great snacks and dinners after practice four times a week, which for a kid like me, with so many other competing mouths in my house, it was a difference maker, especially because we never had snacks at home. I didn't want to give up on the dinners with my teammates after practice which were the best part of my whole day because it was so different, and free and we could talk and laugh loudly without anybody staring at me with a set of bright blue eyes thru a tiny glass and rusty window above the dining table while taking a crap while standing on top of the fucking toilet bowl.

I could talk about anything, I was with a team and with people who liked my companionship and respected me, even though I paid a hefty price to earn their respect. But my desire for challenges and to compete and learn was bigger than being comfortable at SESI. Perhaps because I saw in that desire my ticket to a different life, a life away from Goiania and all that drama. I was curious, ambitious and hungry for challenges and learning, and I knew that if I wanted to become a better player and person, moving on to the best school and the best team in town was the way to go, even if I was reluctant in doing so, I accepted the offer.

If it ain't broke, break it...

The most interesting aspect of this entire situation was that my family had no idea what I was really doing and how good or bad I was as a basketball player. I think they were happy that they didn't have to deal with me in the afternoons and didn't have to worry about me falling from a tree or having to feed me, I guess. They actually didn't really believe that I was offered a scholarship to the most prestigious and most expensive school in our city. Only the rich, smart, and well to do kids attended Colegio Objetivo, not kids like my brothers and sisters and definitely not a kid like me, the skinny, mal nourished with no prospects of any kind who just failed 7th grade not too long-ago type of fella.

I thought it was funny that my family didn't even react to the news that I would be changing schools from an inexpressive public one to a prestigious and expensive private school and no money was going to be needed...that was so out of our reality and so foreign to all of us.

"Wow, what a deal, I felt like I had won the lottery...and I did." That was my thinking and my belief.

At Colegio Objetivo I struggled at first. Everyone had a car, nice clothes and shoes, and money for food at recess. I felt literately like a fish out of water and the social economic pressures got intensified to a level I didn't understand. I walked from home to school which, thank god, wasn't any further than my last school and no hills or ferocious dogs to avoid during my daily journeys.

Just a few months before I transferred to Colegio Objetivo, I was leaving my old school one day and I was attacked and mulled by a big female Rough Collie right outside the school front gate and not only did that fucking dog scared me senseless, the bitch went for my 'pesticles' in a ferocious way and almost ripped my yet to be discovered 'meat and potatoes' off of me. It became very complicated to explain to everyone what had happened and not that I needed another episode of bad luck to have people poke fun at my misery.

I knew a pharmacy close by and Mr. Fonseca the owner and pharmacist in charge always looked at me funny while I'd jumped on the scale daily on my way to school to see if I had gained any weight. I'd never gained a kilogram, nor did I ever buy anything from Mr. Fonseca's pharmacy and given the way he looked at me every day, I knew he didn't appreciate my visits.

Now, Mr. Fonseca is given me a different look and it is fucked up when you get bitten on your penis and testicles and the pharmacist looks at you with that funny look on his face, almost taking pleasure on asking the question:

"What were you poking around with your junk? Are you fucking with me Lenox?" Mr. Fonseca asked me with a grim on his face taking pleasure at my expense.

"No Mr. Fonseca, I am not fucking with you, I was attacked by a vicious dog right outside school a few minutes ago and this is where she bit me." I replied with a tone of annoyance about his attitude towards my pain and suffering.

He gave me an injection for rabies and few meds to take home and told me it was going to be very painful for a few days and that I didn't have to pay him which I was surprised and thankful for his generosity because paying him was the last thing in my mind. I wasn't able go to school for a few days because I couldn't pee without screaming with the burning sensation due to the swelling on my penis, and I wasn't about to give those motherfuckers in school more fodder for their amusement and entertainment. In the bright side of things, if there was such a thing, when that dog almost castrated me and bit my dick off, I learned a valuable lesson to always protect my privates at all costs on the basketball court, not to mention next time I felt threatened by perverted animals during the different routes I had to walk to and from the new school.

Perhaps that dick bite was Zippy reincarnated in a female mut getting back at me for leaving him all alone in the middle of the Amazon Forest with the boa constrictors, now taking pleasure at my pain and misery and saying; "take that motherfucker, we are even now."

After that freaky incident, I was super aware of every dog in the neighborhood and my new path to school consisted of zig zagging my skinny frame thru the different streets and avoiding by all means any encounter with a four legged creature, even those behind the fancy walls and secured gates on my way to and from school because with my good luck; it wouldn't be too far-fetched for one of those fucking creatures to jump over the fence in search of my bones again, literately.

CHAPTER XI
About Fucking Time!

After I accepted the scholarship and transferred to the fancy Colegio Objetivo, things started to get a bit more normalized once I made a couple of friends who I felt had a few things in common with me. I met this flabby looking kid named Lourival, which by coincidence had the same name of one of my new teammates at the new club and is still one of my best friends today, Lourival Ferreira Bernades.

Lourival Marques however was the son of two university professors and had a sister named Carla who was much older than me but unexpectedly, became the biggest crush of my 14 years on planet earth. She had long and wavy hair which she always wore it down and she was so nice to me that I thought she had a crush on me just as well. Lourival Marques was exactly the type of friend I needed at that stage in my life, he helped me get acquainted with the new school and made me feel normal amongst all those rich and smart kids at Colegio Objetivo. His family seemed rich to me because they had a nice apartment, a nice car (a blue VW Variante, station wagon type) great food every time I visited with them and less kids than my household.

We sat next to each other at school in this theater like seating arrangement type of classroom where the teacher lectured from this platform below and the students sat in rolls from high to low like a movie theater. It was very different to me from the single school chair/table I was used to at all the previous public schools I attended. The seats were fancy and comfortable, and the classroom had air conditioning which it was something I had never experienced before at home, in a car or school which was very welcome during those steaming hot Goiania summers.

Lourival and I sat all the way in the back at the highest roll of the classroom because I was too tall and got tired of hearing the whispers and complaining from people behind me that they couldn't see what the teacher was writing on the chock board because my head was on their way. In the back of the classroom, we felt like kings of the joint, we were above everyone else and we could see everything that was happening down below. The way the class rotation worked was the students stayed in their assigned classrooms and the teachers move around from classroom to classroom for each of their hour lesson of their respective subject: Chemistry, Physics, Math, Portuguese (writing and literature), English (as a second language), Geography and History. These were the subjects we study and besides Chemistry, Physics and English, I had no problems with anything else, not even math. The seats were so close to each other and the classroom so big with about 35 to 40 students each that if I had any problems, I could always peek at Lourival's work and he'd bail me out. I wasn't cheating, just working in collaboration with my bestie because he, being the nerd he was and son of two intellectuals, had no problems with any of the subjects in school and he was excellent in English which I couldn't even say "yes, "no," or "Macdonald's."

Lourival Marques and I became inseparable friends, and we did homework together at his house, we went to the library when needed, spent time together during recess and were best pals. He'd never came to my house though, but I don't think I ever invited him anyways. Perhaps unconsciously I was too embarrassed of my neighborhood, my house and lifestyle. We were also meeting at Clube Jao where his family were members, and he would get weekend passes for me to join him and play basketball together.

Clube Jao was far away from where I live so I would jump on the bus (thru the back door - for free) going towards the club and jump off at the intersection which would have a fork on the road that would lead to the city's airport to the left and to Clube Jao to the right as the final destination. Since I didn't have any money for the bus ride and the buses to the club where too far in between, I'd jump off at the intersection and either walked or hitch hike all the way to the club on the weekends when I got the passes from my new friend. Most people in their nice cars would only be taking that road to either go to their fancy homes near the gated community where Clube Jao was located or to the Club itself, so getting a ride wasn't very difficult and people were nice. I'd hitch hike there and back to my house and jump off as close as I could to home and walk the rest of the way, walking is and has always been very familiar and therapeutic to me.

At club Jao, there were many pick-up games during the weekends, specially, on Saturday mornings. Some of the best players in town would come down to play on an uncovered court while a bunch of other players and spectators watched and waited for next and their chance to show their talents. The winners would stay on till they lost and when that happened some of the better players on the losing team would get picked up again because nobody wanted to lose and wait for hours before they get back on the court again. I was one of the first players to be picked by the team captains and whatever team I played for; we'd would win most of the time. I was dominant on those pick-up games, and everyone wanted to have me on their team. I felt wanted and important, and I would play till there was nobody else to play with, whether be a 5 on 5, 2 on 2 or 1 on 1…as long as someone wanted to play, I would play and play hard all the time. The teams I played on had the best winning record in that club and the scores were posted in the main lobby for everyone to see.

Lourival Marques would play a bit, but he wasn't that good of a player, he was out of shape and very slow and I stopped feeling bad because the other players wouldn't pick him to play. Sometimes he'd stay and watch the games for hours without ever putting a foot on the court and every now and then he'd get a chance to mix it up with everyone else when there weren't enough players. Perhaps he was playing through me, his best pal who was always on the court and winning often, perhaps he were both living our lives and passions through each other, him vicariously living his basketball ambitions through me and me through him in school where he excelled at levels I couldn't fathom. Fair exchange I say, but I doubt that my overthinking here is granted, we had no idea what we were doing than, and I am not sure those thoughts were in his mind, but I have always been a protector of the weak, a Robin Hood of sorts for lack of a better description and I wanted him to be picked and play but I was never one of the captains because that was a privilege for the older players and not for a 14 year old skinny kid.

I spent lots of time with Lourival Marques and created many memorable moments in our two years together at Colegio Objetivo. In one of our many adventures we embarked on, I told Lourival that I had an aunt who owned a nice farm in Bela Vista, a tiny town 50 kilometers south of Goiania, and that my aunt Justina was never at the farm during the weekdays and perhaps we could skip school one day and go to the farm to pick some jaboticaba, a delicious round grape size Brazilian fruit plentiful at my aunt's farm.

He liked the idea, and the fruit was in season and we both loved the sweet taste of those black tropical hard skin grapes which are sold even to this day in every corner and stop light in Goiania. He said that he had a neighbor and friend named Gael and his grandmother had a Brasilia (another small VW type of station wagon) seating in the garage and that we could perhaps borrow it for a day and venture out to the farm. I thought his idea was rad and loved his thinking and his adventurous spirit which was somewhat surprising to me because not only was he a nerd, but he also looked like one of those shy and reserved personality types and I didn't know he had that wild side in him. He had no fear and was the coolest of my friends; smart, caring, calm and collected, good student, good son and friend and he was brave, courageous and a fucking wild beast of a kid.

"Great, let's do it but the problem is none of us really know how to drive, do we?" I asked rhetorically with a grin in my face.

I have been observing my father driving and was obsessed and in awe with how good of a driver he was. He'd put his left elbow hanging outside the window, he would open the small triangular wind breaker on the1600cc VW TL he was now driving, which belonged to his boss at the mechanic shop he's been moonlighting after his taxi driver shifts were finished. I knew how to change the gears from seating on the driver's seat of the VW TL and pretend I was driving to my own farm with my farmer's hat on, looking at all the cattle and the fruit trees while my family would be watching me in awe of how cool I look on the driving seat till I snap out of it or till my dad scream at me to clean the windows inside and not to forget to clean the dashboard because his boss liked his cars clean and spotless. Washing my father's boss's car on Sunday afternoons after the best meal of the week and the Formula 1 races, was the closest I would ever get to driving it.

So, on a Tuesday morning after we all pretended to be going to school, we met up at Gael's grandmother's garage downstairs and decided that we would grab a few empty buckets and take his grandmother's VW to the farm and have some fun. I think the jaboticaba was the last thing in our minds, we just wanted to be wild and see if we could do it without destroying the car or killing anyone in the process. We started with Gael driving in the city which he handled better than I expected with a few mistakes which almost left the transmission on the pavement and the clutch burnt out couple of times. We were so happy, so free and with such sense of accomplishment that it didn't matter how many red lights we ran thru, or how many times the car jerked up and down for being on the wrong gear or off the clutch too soon, we'd poke fun of whoever was driving and gave each other tips on how and when to release the clutch or when to turn the blinkers on. We were giggling the entire time and glad we were doing it and decided not to talk about getting caught by the police or our families for skipping school. We agreed to deal with the consequences later and decided to just enjoy the ride and help each other during each of our turn on the wheel because neither one of us were any good at driving although we've been yearning for a long time, but our parents thought we were too young to be learning how to drive.

Once we got out of the city, there were about 40 kilometers of dirt road which I volunteered to drive on because I had seen my father manage that type of driving many times and I was confident I could do it. We didn't have to go fast, and I felt a bit safer than the city driving. We all agreed to that and Lourival shared the dirt road responsibilities with me for a few kilometers, but he was just happy to be there, to be skipping school and doing something really fun which he lacked in his apartment life complex where he lived, and he didn't have young kids, siblings his age or friends around.

We made it to the farm old front gate without any hick ups except for the clutch and transmission mishaps along the way, but nothing too major to speak of. When we got close to the farm, it started to rain a little but I had visited a few times with my cousin Adriano and his family, I recognized the entire landscape and where to go so I took the wheel again and drove thru the rain, the ravines, rivers, creeks, mountains and meadows, plenty of cattle and horses along the way filled our lungs with the smells of farm land, cattle manure, wild flowers, and the ever so distinguishing aroma of wet dirt roads and all the smells our senses bring to the forefront when you are feeling invincible. That's how I felt, invincible.

"I am fucking driving with no one around to pick and/or yell at me and about to get some incredible sweet treats to eat on our way back... fucking invincible!" I always knew it would feel good to drive but I didn't realize it could be that liberating and so influential for the rest of my life.

When we got to the farm, things seemed to be as I thought they would, there wasn't anybody around and I guided the boys with the empty five-gallon buckets we brought to collect jaboticaba from the hundreds of fruit trees that were loaded with the round black marble looking fruit which you eat it by squeezing the white juicy meat in your mouth and throwing away the hard black skin. Almost like a lychee except smaller and softer.

We were in heaven for there were so many trees at a perfect height to be picked without much effort and lined up for hundreds of feet to the right and left of us. The Jaboticaba was perfectly ripe and plentiful, more than we could eat or collect in the five-gallon buckets. We had so much fun and completely lost track of time by jumping from one tree to the next and eating the sweet treat and picking more of it for our journey back.

Suddenly, we heard noises, a metal clacking of sorts and sounded like someone was talking to an animal. Somebody had arrived at the farm, and I got desperate because I never asked my aunt if we could be there on our own, specially, given that we were all 14-year-old kids driving more 50 kilometers from the city on a stolen VW from Gael's granny to steal fruits from a family member, that didn't sound like such a good idea anymore. I wasn't feeling that invincible now!

It turned out a nearby neighbor farmer heard us driving by and came by to check on what we were up to. The only think that came to my mind was: "I am literately going to get killed by my father because this is going to get to his ears without a doubt." So, I took my farmer's hat off and put on my fictitious actor's hat on and went out to meet the party pooper neighbor who was spoiling our day.

"Howdy there, how are you?" Said Lenox.

"Houdy! I'm mighty fine but what you boys up to"? Reply the neighbor.

"Oh, auntie Justina and uncle Joao went to Bela Vista to attend a cattle auction and they should be back in couple of hours. They asked us to stay back and fill up couple of buckets with jaboticabas to bring home" I replied but uncertain he bought my story.

"Please come in for some coffee, they shouldn't take long." I insisted, hoping he would be convinced we were with family and leave.

"Thanks for the invite but I have to go, please say hello to your uncle and aunt for me." Replied the neighbor still with a suspicious look on his wrinkled face or perhaps it was just my guilty mind playing tricks on me…again.

I went to the back of the barn and threw up all the jaboticaba I had eaten in the last 30 minutes since we had arrived there. I was so afraid of getting caught that I got an upset stomach with the thought of not just having to deal with my father if he found out but also my aunt and uncle who were my bosses at LBA. I took a big and unnecessary risk for sure, but my life was complicated with so many weird feelings and confusion that I enjoyed the adrenaline rush, the possibility of getting away with it and, the thrill of adventure those risks represented.

We collected as much fruits as we could in our buckets and got out of there in a hurry. We made it back home in half the time it took us to get there and were scared shitless of getting pulled over by cops and getting caught by our parents (at least I was). If my father found out I skipped school with my friends and drove in someone else's stolen car thru the city and thru the highway, thru two highway patrol police stations along the side of the dirt road to steal fruits from my aunt's/boss's farm; the cemetery was the only destination for my sorry, skinny, buck toothed, afro haired, zit faced, no ass carcasses.

Miraculously, somehow, someway, nobody ever found out we were there or if they did, I never heard anything about it…lucky young fella I was and perhaps my luck was starting change.

"About fucking time!!!" I thought.

The experience of driving a car has always been one which intrigued me my entire childhood. I would observe how my father drove and all the details and mannerisms he had from the time he opened the driver's door to the moment he turned the car off and always gently and softly shut the door. I was fascinated by all the mirror fixing every single time, and never really understood the ritual since my dad was the only person who drove his cars (or his boss's car) in our house. None of my sisters or my stepmom ever learned how to drive with my father, he had no desire or patience to teach anyone, besides none of us were brave enough to ask or wanted to take lessons from him and be yelled at for making mistakes.

He would get in the car, adjust the seat, adjust the rearview mirror, the side mirrors, he would then stretch his left arm out and pull the radio antenna all the way up and rotate the dial on the radio till there was no static and on his favorite Radio Brasil Central 1270 AM sports station, the same radio station and location where I fessed up in that rainy and muggy day about failing 7th grade. He would then push the cigarette lighter in while reaching for a packet of his beloved Hollywood cigarettes on the left pocket of his shirt, hold the packet with his right hand, tap the bottom of the packet onto his left palm three times, brake the golden plastic seal by picking it with his fingernail, take one cigarette out and before he lit it up, he would massage it and roll it on his fingers as if he was rolling a joint. He'd open the little triangular shaped windbreaker window to a certain angle so to keep the wind blowing inside the car, take the cigarette lighter still burning red hot, lit up his cigarette, take a long puff and all that smoke in thru his mouth and out thru his nose in one big exhale as if he was taking his last breath. The little triangular wind breaker window served as air conditioning and circulated the hot and smoky air inside the car. I am surprised I never picked up the smoking habit because my father smoked often, and I never minded the smell of his cigarettes than as much as I detest it now. Two packs a day was his average, he did it till he was 50 years old when he decided to quit at once, cold turkey. There were no patches, no doctors, no therapist, no mind tricking fucking doctrines and he was as addicted as anyone I have ever met but, when he made up his mind that he wouldn't smoke anymore, he never did.

CHAPTER XII
Shift Happens!

I struggled with some family members and friends who say they can't never stop smoking and that smoking is a disease and needs medical treatment. Ok, I get that, I understand that everyone is different and wired in a particular way but somehow I tend to fall in the category of "I can do whatever I put my mind to," and since I never had any vices or addictions in my life, unless of course you consider dramas, and motorcycles an addiction that is?!?! I get frustrated with my brother and brother-in- law and a few friends, when I see them smoking and telling everyone they can't quit because it's a disease and they don't have the mental strength to stop it even though they really want to. That's an excuse if you ask me but what the hell do I know except for the experiences I had with my father and other people who quit cold turkey cigarettes, alcohol, drugs, sex, prescription drugs, and all kinds of other vices imaginable?

My father loved fishing, hunting, loved his cigarettes and his womanizing ways and in a confusing and twisted way, he loved his family too. He would spend some of his Sundays working on his car which he had always kept clean and in great shape. He would take out the carburetor and dismantle it in its tiniest parts and clean the whole thing with gasoline already half way full in a cut out small plastic bucket where he'd soak the tiny parts into. Next, he'd take an old toothbrush and clean each of those parts and blow inside the tiny holes to make sure there wasn't anything that could impede the carburetor to work perfectly smooth and get the best possible gas mileage. Every penny saved was important and I understood why.

I was always mesmerized by how particular and detail oriented he was with the engines albeit cars, boats, planes, trucks, tractors, marine or otherwise engines, My father was the best there was and I wish he had taught me how to do those things because he looked so smart and in such a state of joy and pleasure while doing it and I completely envied his mechanic skills…except for when he needed us kids to grab something for him and we couldn't find it. In those moments hell would break lose but I still loved watching him. I shouldn't be surprised obviously because that's how he made his leaving as a taxi driver and a mechanic. With eight kids and a wife to feed, he couldn't afford downtime and being handy was imperative. I wish however, that my old man took care of his family with the same gentleness, love, kindness and passion he took care of his car (which wasn't even his at that time) and his tools. I guess cars and tools don't have report cards, run up phone bills, don't require daily food or emotional nurturing.

On Saturdays my father would work half day till 2 or 3pm and he would come home and work on his fishing gear in preparation for his fishing trips to nearby rivers around that part of the country. He would dig some areas in our backyard in search for earth worms which he used for bait. That part of our lives was very pleasant and exciting even though I wasn't really into fishing. I always enjoyed the trips even if I never really caught any fish which was usually the case. I never really had too much patience as a kid to seat there and fish all day under a hot, muggy and mosquito infested fishing holes my father would commit to. I went for the food instead, which consisted of rice, beans (feijao tropeiro) made by my father's best friend and fishing aficionado Joao Raimundo. There were also cabob steaks grilled on charcoal my father would make from wood he'd collect for that specific occasion. Sometimes he would send us thru the bushes to collect dry sticks to help start the fire and invariably we'd bump into small snakes which were always a thrill because my brother and I would start screaming and ran back to camp site only to see my father take out his 22 caliper Beretta revolver and ask us to show him where it was. He'd shoot it on its head and laugh while holding it on his hand and joking about the size of it. That whole scene, the smells of the charcoal and the sticks we threw on the fire pit he'd made to keep predators out and warm up our food, the beans and rice and the soft tapioca root slowed cooked the night before and melting in the old copper pan, the fresh tobacco rolled up in dried leaves they smoke and the whole atmosphere, it was heaven to me, especially because I could experience my father in nature and in nature he was fun and kind. I could see my father was happy in that environment, he was gentle and loving and often took the time to teach us how to shoot his Beretta revolver, show where the fish was biting and how to hook the earth worm on the small hook without destroying the bait.

"If you start from his ass and keep pushing it thru the hook, when you get close to its head do a double poke thru its body and its head will be dangling from the hook, guarantee you will catch a big one son." He would explain it in detail, and with great pride. I've always appreciated the time he took to teach us and passing on the knowledge.

It was a special occasion to learn from my old man about fishing and nature and top of that, I could eat as much as I wanted because there wasn't anybody else we needed to share the food with besides my younger brother Cesar who didn't eat much. My father and Joao Raimundo were there to fish, drink the entire bottle of their beloved 51 cachaça and smoke their aromatic tobacco, not to eat. We would spend the night before preparing for that fishing trip and that was just as much fun as the fishing trip itself. My father would already be in a great mood, and he always had little treats for us like candy, chocolate, and crispy fried pig skin (torresmo) which he'd made it himself in hot oil from small pig's belly chunks he'd bought at the butcher next to serial killer Antonio's barber shop. My father never really slept before those fishing trips, he'd stay up all night cleaning and meticulously separating his fishing gear, preparing the food, the charcoal, the bait needed to be fresh and covered on fresh dirt from the back yard and he needed to have a bottle of cachaça to share with Joao Raimundo throughout the day. He lubed his fishing reels for the bigger fish and prepared all the bamboo fishing sticks for the small fish. Lastly but not least, he'd spent a great amount of time cleaning his Beretta revolver for the inevitable encounter with reptiles and animals in that part of the world, a gun which he always had with him in every fishing trip we went.

My brother and I would go to bed late and very excited to be woken up early by father at 4am those Sundays to get to the river before sunrise. My father would look for the right fishing spots where he could seat on a rock and fish all day, but also a place where he could make a fire pit, put his charcoal in the pit and make sure there was a seating area for lunch time which usually occurred much later than I wanted. For the most part I would spend my time throwing rocks in the river and waiting for the awesome meal I was about to have, and I would only be fishing when the fish was biting or when my father put a stick in my hand, and he'd tell me:

"Cast your line right there Lenox, you will catch a good one for lunch." He'd be pointing to a fishing hole where he knew the fish was biting and inevitably it did.

In the meantime, Joao Raimundo and my brother Cesar could stay all day on the same spot even if they never got a single bite or caught anything, they were patient and beautiful to watch how skillful they were and how much they enjoyed that whole experience. I on the other hand enjoyed the experience of watching their experience and was in constant awe of their skills and their resolve to catch fish which they always did. I could seat on the same spot sometimes and do exactly the same thing and have the exact same bait and catch nothing while they were reeling them in one after the other.

I never really understood that kind of patience but over the years I have learned to appreciate that fishing isn't about the fish, but rather about being in the moment in time, in the present with beautiful and quiet nature, meditative and therapeutic for some, agonizing and terrifying for others.

In one of those weekends, my father announced on Friday that we were going fishing on Sunday, and I asked him if I could stay home that weekend.

"Why don't you want to go fishing Lenox?" Asked my father in a very inquisitive and surprised tone of voice.

"I am not feeling well and have a headache." Said Lenox fearful of what the response would be.

My sisters were puzzled and so was my brother because up till then, I had never missed a single fishing trip and I loved it even though I wasn't as crazy about staying under the hot son for hours on end like they were.

I had a plan though, I wanted to learn how to drive, and my dad had no patience or the desire to teach me, so I decided to take matters on my own hands.

As usual, they left early morning and I also knew that my sisters and my stepmom Nida were going to spend the day at my aunt's house to attend a birthday party for one of my cousins. We had a birthday party to attend every weekend seemed like and I wasn't very fond of them. So, I asked my sisters to stay home with the excuse that I wasn't feeling very good with cold symptoms. They didn't care at all, and I think it was because they knew I wasn't comfortable around people and parties; besides, they wouldn't have to worry about me seating on a corner waiting for the food to be served and then bugging them about what time we would be going back home.

"Fine, just stay back home and we will see you later this evening." Said Marina with a motherly voice and not at all suspicious of my intentions.

That week my father had been driving a work truck his boss allowed him to use occasionally when he had big engines or machinery to take care of and transport it to the shop. He left the VW TL in the garage, and I had been plotting my weekend in detail the entire week once I learned he was driving the company's truck. My plan was to take that VW out and get myself some fun while learning how to drive around the neighborhood.

There wasn't anybody home so I took my time to walk around the car, opened the hood and did the things my father would usually do before he turned his cars on in the morning by putting some gas in the carburetor and letting the car run for a bit. I did everything I watched him do so many times by the book, and I was proud of myself for remembering all the nuances and details I have been observing for so many years and better yet, everything worked out as planned; there was nobody home, the car was running smoothly once I prepped the carburetor with some gasoline…I was ready to take that bad boy for a spin. I had been dreaming about this day for a long time, I wanted to drive on my own and I couldn't wait to put my left elbow out of the window, crack that triangular wind breaker in a 45-degree angle for ventilation, pull the antenna up, turn the radio on a sports station, fix the mirrors and driver seat, press my foot on the clutch and rev up the 1600cc VW engine. I wanted to change the gears in a smooth motion while holding the steering wheel with the tip of my left fingers, just like my father used to do. This was my chance, and I was going to take it.

Once I got inside the car after going through the warmup routine I'd repeatedly witnessed, I realized I had no idea how to put it on reverse and move it out of the garage, I guess I've missed that lesson and it was a lot more difficult than I anticipated. Each time I tried to reverse it, once I release the clutch the VW TL would come to a weird motion which I had never experienced before while watching my dad driving it; the car would jump in an up and down motion very much like the bulls in the rodeos I was used to watch at the farm fare and I wasn't sure what I was doing wrong. I had only driven once during that adventure trip to my aunt's farm with my friends, but I didn't have to put it on reserve, and I pretty much drove that one time in a straight line on dirt roads, not in the city.

After a few unsuccessful attempts to reverse it, I decided to put the car on neutral and pushed it towards the street with the hopes I could drive it without putting on reverse. I was starting to second guess my plan and wishing I had gone fishing instead. The fucking thing was too heavy for my weak frame to push it to the other side of the street and the VW TL was now one half blocking the sidewalk and the other half was on the street at the mercy of other cars making that tight and sharp corner where our house was located,

"Fuck, I didn't push it hard enough, what do I do now?" Said Lenox with a look of uncertainty on his face.

I looked around to see if I could find help and push the car back into the garage to abort the mission when I saw Lazaro, one of our neighbors across the street who was seating on the curbside while people watching on the sidewalk immediately across the street from my house. I walked over and told him I needed some help on getting my father's car back in the garage.

"Hi Lazaro, I inadvertently put the car on reverse while washing it and I am stuck, can you help me?" Asked Lenox while pointing to the direction of where the VW was.

"Ok!" replied Lazaro without hesitating.

He came over and helped me push the car back into the garage and when I thanked him and asked if he knew how to drive, he said he did, but he didn't have a car, which I knew that was the case because all neighbors around my house were just as poor as we were and didn't have cars themselves. A few had carriages with old horses to pull it or Vespas and bicycles but not cars.

"Would you be interested in driving with me around the block?" Lenox asked reluctantly.

"Lenox, are you serious? Everyone knows your father is a madman and are you sure he's ok with you driving." Asked Lazaro with a lot of reluctancy after hearing my proposal.

"Yes, my father is sleeping, and he knows about it." Replied Lenox.

"Are you mad Lenox? Are you fucking crazy? Everyone knows your father's reputation and the loud fights that happens in your house almost daily which everyone around can hear it." Said Lazaro abruptly.

"Can you guys hear the fights and shouting?" Asked Lenox, embarrassed.

"Yes Lenox, we can hear everything, and everyone knows your old man loses his shit with you guys in a daily basis…we can hear everything." Lazaro said unapologetically.

I said I was serious and that my father was ok with it and that he was sleeping inside the house. I don't think he believed me, but perhaps he too was looking for something to do that Sunday morning because there wasn't much action for him to watch while just seating there on the curb. He obliged and off we went. He took the wheel first and showed me how to put it in reverse, how to make a smooth transition from the clutch to the gas pedal and it seemed easy for him to reverse it out of the garage without having the feeling of riding a bull with a strap squishing its balls. We took it around our block couple of times without any mistakes and I was honestly impressed with Lazaro's driving skills. When we got in front of my house again, he stopped right on the corner where we always played our soccer and basketball games, and he could see and feel my anxiety about being next.

"Can I try it now?" I said impatiently while salivating with the prospects of being behind the wheel…finally!

"Yes, but go easy on the clutch, that's the most important thing and DO NOT use your left foot on the brake pedal, that can be dangerous." Lazaro emphasized the importance of using the correct foot on each pedal.

"Ok, I got it." Super excited and happy to finally be driving in the city for the first time I was.

I started pretty good, adjusted all the mirrors, the seat, the windows, took a big breath (no cigarettes though) and dove into the experience with all my heart as if this was the best thing ever, and it was. I was hooked immediately, and I am still hooked to this day. I always wanted to be a Formula 1 driver, and this was my initiation. We went couple of times around the block repeating the same route Lazaro had done a few minutes before and then I decided to go a bit further after feeling confident and on top of the world. Left elbow hanging out the open window, right hand on top of the shifter, left hand lightly on top of the steering wheel and I felt like Mario Andretti, one of those famous race car drivers with all the gorgeous women, fancy boats and beautiful families. The only thing I didn't have that reminded me of my father driver habits was the Holywood cigarette on my left fingers.

"Wow Lenox, you never drove before?" Asked Lazaro with a surprise look on his face.

"Well, not in the city like this. I drove one time with a few friends on dirt roads but didn't have to make many turns or deal with other cars or traffic signals and pedestrians around, and didn't have to put on reserve." Said Lenox proud of his driving and happy he didn't go fishing with his father.

I felt like I was meant for driving, it was easy, and I was in my element. We took a couple of laps around a few blocks a bit further from my house and Lazaro said he needed to go home. I said I would drive him back and would continue by myself which he didn't think it was a good idea.

I told him not to worry and to please not to tell anyone he helped me even though my father had said it was ok for me to be driving. We came down on Rua 217 towards my house and Lazaro's place was just across the street around the corner from ours.

"You are a natural Lenox, you are a fucking natural behind the wheel kid!" He said with a sense of pride as my first driving instructor not knowing that I have attentively been observing my father for years and years.

I drove in front of the bakery where I'd often forgotten my bicycle and also in front of "Bar do Benzinho," which is right across from the bakery and where we would get roasted chicken and An one litre bottle size of Coca-Cola on a very special occasion when my old man was in a good mood. I was feeling like a million dollar, dreaming about the McLarens, Ferraris and Lotus formula 1 race cars I might get to drive one day. Cars were a sign of wealth and class in my view, and I spent way too much time envying anyone who had a nice car and wishing I could be as happy as they were.

As we drove down my street from the bakery and right in front of my house which was located on the corner of Rua 217 and Rua 200 where Lazaro lived, I needed to turn right to drop Lazaro off at his house across the street and then would continue by myself as planned. I turned the right blinkers on, press on the clutch in a very control and smooth motion, bleeped it and downshifted to third then second gear, slowing the car down now lightly on the brakes. I was very confident and knew the traffic flow well on that street corner from playing soccer and basketball there my entire life. As I approach that turn, I noticed on the corner of my right eye a little girl on her pink bicycle still on the sidewalk waiting to cross the dangerous corner. In a blink, she pedaled her bike onto the street and crossed right in front of me as I was making my right turn. I don't know what happened exactly, but I must have mixed up the clutch and gas pedals with the wrong foot and I swerved left and away from her and instead of stepping on the brake pedal, I panicked and floored the gas pedal. The old VW TL went straight into a wall immediately across the corner, I saw a wooden bench and at a quick glance, I noticed a woman seating on it holding her child, I was going straight at them. I couldn't stop the car and I plowed hard onto that bench and the cement wall holding Dona Maria's metal gate, which was completely destroyed, the wooden bench exploded into small pieces, chunks of cement were all over the windshield and even inside the car, and the rear-engine VW TL front end was now a bunch of twisted and broken sheet metal in the form a huge V from hitting that cement corner wall.

"Nooooooooo, fuuuuuuuuck!" Said Lenox with tears rolling down his face.

I guess these types of events make one believe in God's existence and his hands on the controls of one's life. It makes us believe in miracles but there I was; 14 years old, in my father's boss' car crashing considerably fast onto a bench while a mother breastfed her child while witnessing the last days of their lives. My life flashed in front of me at lighting speeds and I knew I was doomed because if this experience didn't kill those two innocent people, or me, my father would... without a doubt. I was sure I'd killed those innocent people seating on that bench and they must have been under the car, mangled into pieces.

"Where are they? What the fuck happened"? Lenox started screaming inside the car in shock.

"What about the girl on the pink bicycle? Did I kill her too?" Lenox mind was inundated with thoughts of the end of his life not to mention all those innocent people.

I blanked out, the whole thing happened in a flash, very much like how people describe accidents when they are lucky enough to survive them..."it happened in a blink."

The car hit the bench first and completely shattered it into small little pieces and destroyed the wall behind the bench I crashed on. The front of the car was now mangled due to the impact on the corner of that wall which had a gate leading into Donna Maria's front yard. I don't remember anything after that, I don't remember how we got the car back in the garage and where and how the lady and her baby were.

"How do I go forward from here? How do I recover? How am I going to get out to this mess?" Lenox knew this accident was going to cause major drama at home.

"I must have killed those people and how selfish of me to quickly start thinking about my punishment when I probably killed a mother and her baby and the little girl on the bicycle? They were just seating there in a cool Sunday afternoon and now they are gone, because of me, yes me, had I gone fishing none of that would've happened." Lenox guilty mind was fucking with him and he couldn't stop crying in complete despair.

Truth is there are no reasonable or plausible answers to all my questions which came to mind in that moment.

"You know what? Fuck it cus I am dead anyways, I might as well either kill myself or run away…again… before my father comes back home and finishes the job." Said Lenox to himself in pure desperation and disbelief about his bad luck.

I heard a loud scream and a bunch of people coming to the accident scene, I heard a baby crying and people murmuring. My friend Lazaro was gone, nowhere to be found and I was still inside that car thinking why the hell was I born? Wishing my mother should have died before she gave birth to me and wondering how come things could go so wrong when I was having such a great time?

"When am I ever going to catch a fucking break?"

Some of the neighbors came to the window of the car and asked me if I was ok and brought me some water. I remembered asking someone I can't remember who, if the woman and her baby and the girl on her bicycle were ok, and they said they were fine and that the woman on the bench saw the car coming towards them and she moved seconds before I hit the bench and the wall. I don't even know if I was relieved to hear that they were ok or if I was so shocked and paralyzed that I couldn't really think about or feel anything, except the fear of my father's rage when he'd return from his fishing trip and sees his boss's car mangled in the garage and our neighbor's wall destroyed. How, what, when, who is going to pay to fix that?

"Somebody will have to pay for that car, the wall, the gate and bench, and we can barely buy food around here." Lenox was repeating it with so much guilt he couldn't even feel relieved that nobody was hurt or killed.

Some of the neighbors had helped me push the car back into the garage and I locked the gate with the padlock my father kept on top of that blue gate. I went inside the house, sat on the cold black and red checkered tile floor in our living room, and cried for hours on end with all kinds of thoughts a child shouldn't be having. The thought of running away and never returning home being the number one choice. I cried till there were no more tears left in me. I went outside in the garage to check on the car a few times which now had the front end mangled beyond recognition and I realized how hard I hit that wall and how lucky I was to not have killed or even hurt anyone and to be alive since I wasn't wearing a seat belt.

I walked across the street to check on the lady and her baby and the girl on the bicycle who was the reason I panicked, but they were nowhere to be found and I was told nobody got hurt in the accident. I checked the wall and the bench and saw the massive destruction I caused and how crazy and lightning-fast life can change. I tried to talk to the lady who was seating on that bench, I wanted to know her name and her child's name, wanted to say I was sorry, but I was told by Dona Maria, her landlord, that she was too traumatized and upset to speak to anyone.

"Who's going to pay to fix my metal gate, my wall and the bench Lenox?" Asked Dona Maria with an embarrassed tone of voice and clearly not wanting to add to my misery.

"I will pay for it ma'am, I will take care of it and I am so sorry." Lenox replied with tears running down his face again.

"How are you going to deal with your father Lenox? Senhor Zeze is a difficult man and not one that will take this lightly." Dona Maria knew my father's short temper and was genuinely concerned for my well-being. I am sure she and the entire neighborhood was concerned because they all had heard the numerous arguments and fights coming from our house with my father screaming his lungs out and this won't be dealt differently.

"I don't know but I am afraid my father might kill me this time around. I am sorry again." I walked towards my house sobbing and I looked down the street and I could see the long stretch of pave road that would go from south to north on Rua 200 and the thought of starting to run away for good and never come back was invading my mind again.

Everything happened so fast and nobody getting hurt was either a miracle, pure luck, an act of God, or my late mother's divine intervention. At least I was looking thru the optics of a silver lining that nobody was hurt and that might have been the big break I had been asking for perhaps. I checked on the woman and her baby again that afternoon, but she didn't want to talk to me, and I never really got to see her again and didn't know who she was because Dona Maria had a bunch of small units she rented to transient people and the woman had just moved into the neighborhood after she gave birth in a hospital nearby, I was told. I didn't know about the thereabouts of her family, her husband or even if she had one but I wanted to give her a hug and ask her name and offer my apologies.

That Sunday was one of the most difficult days I had experienced in my life and once I knew that everyone was ok, I started to think about the inevitable, how to tell my father once he gets home. That afternoon I never felt more alone than any other time in my life, and no other day in my life to that point had been so streteched out and soooooooo fucking long.

To my surprise, my sister Marina came home early around 4pm to change her clothes because she wanted to go see a movie with our cousin Miriam. I was seating in the front porch and surprised and shocked to see her because I wasn't prepared to talk to anyone. I didn't have the courage to tell her because there was nothing she could do, and I wasn't about to destroy her Sunday afternoon as well. Or perhaps, I was just fucking afraid of what she might do to me as she too was a brute sometimes being the oldest and responsible sister and becoming the mother of four younger children at age of 14 after my mom died. I didn't say anything and when she asked me if I wanted to go to the movies with them and have ice cream afterwards, I didn't even wait till she finished her sentence.

"YES, I want that." Replied Lenox.

Marina was surprised to my quick answer for I had no idea what movie we were about to see, I had been to the movies once in 1974 to watch Herbie Rides Again, the second of the Love Bug movie franchise, and I never forgot how fun the experience to seat in the dark and watch a movie on a huge screen was. I felt wealthy and was hooked on the silver screen forever and still am to his day. I didn't get to see movies at the theatres hardly ever because we couldn't afford it and we only had one theater in Goiania.

The movie in that macabre afternoon was Kramer vs. Kramer with Dustin Hoffman and Meryl Streep and besides being a great drama of divorce, and fights over things and children between parents and the senseless laws that surround divorce in the United States, it was what I needed and the perfect outlet for the occasion. I couldn't stop thinking about how to find a way to tell my sister what happened and what to expect of my father who in a few hours will be home from his fishing trip and most likely a little tipsy.

I cried for the entire duration of the movie, from the time I sat on my chair to the time we got up to leave but my sister Marina and my cousin Miriam didn't notice anything and if they did, they kept it to themselves and perhaps felt I really got into the sappy story and the great acting of my favorite actress of all time and the only woman I would give an arm and a leg to spend the rest of my life with; Merryl Strip. I was in love with her and still am to this moment in time. It was a very small and only theater in town, and I wasn't used to that kind of pitch black darkness. The place was packed so I felt it was the perfect setting for me to unleash my incessant and uninterrupted crying and unload my anxiety for what was about to unfold.

When the movie was over, Miriam asked me if I wanted ice cream and I immediately said another resounding YES! I love ice cream and there was a particular place which I only dreamt about having one of those ginormous banana splits and never had the money to do it. The ice cream shop was called "Fonte do Paladar" and it was within walking distance from the theater. I heard from a few of my well to do school mates that this place had an incredibly large banana split filled with chocolate, whipped cream, and roasted peanuts on top.

"I want one of those." I told our cousin Mirian pointing to the gigantic banana split on the huge menu on the wall while my sister was trying to stop me.

"That's too big and too expensive Lenox, just get one scoop of your favorite flavor." Marina said with embarrassment in her voice.

Miriam said it was ok and if it was too big, they could share it with me. For the first time in my life, I felt like demanding something, probably out of frustration or perhaps the rampant fear running in my head that this treat might be the last one of my short-lived life, so fuck it…let's go medieval on this rare motherfucker ice cream moment and get the biggest and most expensive one in the menu.

"Nope, I don't want to share it and I want that banana split with everything on top, please…thanks!" I said confidently.

I grabbed the oval shaped dish which was spilling over with the delicious hot chocolate sauce and the homemade whipped cream all over the edges. I walked outside the shop and sat in a small table which only had one chair while they were deciding what to get for themselves. I didn't want to talk or think, I just wanted to enjoy that moment of solitude and the sweetness of that frozen treat and perhaps freeze my brain, my thoughts, my feelings of inadequacy, my inferiority complex, my discuss with my overgrown bones and protruded body parts which reminded me every second of how unattractive, and how fucking unlucky I have been so far in life.

"This is my redemption, I will savor every fucking bite as if it was my last, and if this is it, this is the feeling I want to go out with; a feeling of having something I desire for so long and was now able to get it, even if under extenuating circumstances." I said to myself while trying to hide the tears.

Brain Freeze! I wanted to freeze my feelings too and everything in that moment in time.

I walked twice in front that ice cream parlor every day, on my way to practice at Joquei Clube and sometimes I'd go in, pretend that I wanted to order one of those bad boys only to change my mind in the middle of the process because I didn't have the money to pay for it, it was expensive and only in my dreams I could have such a gigantic treat.

Now, I was seating there with one of them treats in front of me and all I could do was think and cry. I couldn't taste the chocolate, the vanilla or the delicious strawberry flavors. I couldn't feel the texture I imagined coming from the thick whipped cream which they claimed was homemade by the owner's grandmother, or even the hot chocolate sauce spilling over the edges. My mind was somewhere else obviously, and my taste buds completely inhibited by the rampant fear of being whooped till bleeding again.

"I rather die and have this Banana split be my last wish before my father returns home." I replied to the many voices in my head all speaking at the same fucking time in suicidal chaos mode and fear of what's about to unfold when King Zeze comes home from his fishing trip after downing an entire bottle of that hard sugar cane stuff.

Such a dramatic kid I was come to think of it.

My sister left me alone even though it was impossible for her and Miriam not to notice my emotional fragility. Nevertheless, it was like they knew what was happening inside of me but didn't want to spoil my moment. They never asked me why I was crying, never questioned why I left half of that delicious banana split basically untouched and melting on the oval crystal dish making a mess on the tiny table. They simply waited for me to be ready to leave, they never came to the table where I was seating and never said anything on the way home.

"Thank you for the banana split and for letting me just be!!!" I said, while looking at both of them.

When Miriam dropped us off at home that evening, it was around 6:30pm or a bit thereafter, the sun was setting, the air was humid and heavy as it is usually the case in Goiania specially on Sundays, that's how Sunday evenings felt like to me; heavy, humid, lacking family love even though I was surrounded by family. I used to cry on Sunday evenings and every Christmas and never really understood why. Sunday evenings felt like the end of something that was never coming back again, and Christmas always felt like I was missing something or perhaps someone who was never there, my mother.

Marina walked inside the house and I sat outside in the "alpendre" (front porch), the same place where I was seating when she came home early a couple of hours ago. I hugged the double skinny, cold cement pillars that supported our house and cried incessantly with the feeling of complete failure and discussed with my luck. My luck to have been born in this poor and disjointed family who struggled so much all the time. A family which seemed at the time to be falling apart with so much abuse, poverty, violence, fights, arguments, confusion, desperation, and drama in every turn and in every corner and I wasn't helping our cause with my constant fuckups and failed attempted adventures that usually turned out badly for everyone and often put our family deeper in the hole.

Well, at least the farm driving one went swell and I should be thankful instead of sorry. Despite my bad luck, I often and perhaps unconsciously tried to look for the silver lining and grab onto some positive things happening in my life which, looking back today, there were plenty of good things, but I was a strange teenager and teenagers are self-centered, dramatic and filled with self-righteousness and rarely see the positive things in life or in themselves.

However, I was constantly conflicted and saddened with the prospect of having to find a way to leave this house and this damn city once and for all and never come back. I was getting tired of crying and the many different feelings running thru my mind were dismantling any chance I had to get through this hell-bent Sunday evening, which is just about to get uglier.

Marina came outside and brought me a cup with cold water she had just gotten from the round shape clay water filter we kept on the upper left side shelve of our small kitchen. I took the glass but dropped it on its way to my mouth and the glass broke into pieces on the cold red cement of our front porch. I was trembling, my hands were shaking, and my lips were purple and shivering incessantly.

"What's wrong with you Lenox? Why have you been crying all afternoon and during the entire movie? You ordered an expensive ice cream and barely touched it. What happened Lenox?" She asked and I could feel her fear of what my answer would be.

"You can talk to me, what happened? I won't tell father anything, I promise you." She continued

I grabbed her hands and tip toed around the broken glass on the cement floor and led her to the garage which was only a few meters away from where I was seating. I walked her all the way around the car to the other side of the garage where she could see the mangled VW TL and she got down on her knees and started to cry with so much sadness that my fear was replaced with guilt, hopelessness, and desperation.

"How could I bring any more problems and more expenses to this house?" I said to her crying and sobbing.

My sisters were all working very odd jobs with the piano lessons, hanger decorations, manicure and pedicure, cake baking and mango selling, and this is how I contributed?

"How could I do this to all of us?" I kept on crying while she covered her face with her hands and let out a loud scream, just as desperate as

I was. She then stood up from her knees and took a closer look at the wrecked VW by walking around a few times and murmuring.

"This car doesn't even belong to father, how is he going to pay for it? Did anybody get hurt? Are you ok, are you hurt? This is going to get ugly Lenox, very ugly. I am sorry." Marina was in tears and pensative while machinating some type of solution to the gigantic challenge in front of us.

I knew everybody will have to pay the same price for my mistake and I felt an immense amount of guilt which, for a 14-year-old who felt pretty fucked up already himself, it wasn't easy to understand, comprehend or try to explain the many feelings raging inside of my dense head.

I told her what happened, and I asked her not to get involved and let me deal with father on my own when he returned home from his fishing trip. I begged her not to tell anyone else and to keep everyone away from the house so the drama would be minimized between me and King Zeze.

She knew just how much our father was careful with his boss's cars and how much he despised anyone going against his orders and not touching his things, his car, his tools, his socks, his Gillette razor blades, his comb, his Johnson oil for his hair, his cachaça, his outboard engines, his aluminum boat, his hand made bbq grills, his pepper jars, his every little and big thing in that fucking house….arghhhhhhhhhhhh I just wanted to scream!!!!!

I went for a walk around our block which I would do often and still do to this day anytime I feel I need space to think and get my shit together. I don't know how long I walked and how far I went but it felt like there was a good opportunity to find the end of the line, find a cliff, open my arms, and just let go and leave all that craziness behind once and for all. There wouldn't be a better time to run away or simply vanish once and for all, everyone would understand it. I just don't want to be beaten and whooped and humiliated again but I understood and accepted that my father had his reasons, plenty of them, after all, that's how things were dealt with at home, with physical punishment and that was understood by everyone.

After walking for a long time seemed like, I turned on 217th street (Rua 217) from 224th street, I noticed something that brought me back to the day my mother died. I noticed all these cars parked on both sides of our street and a feeling of dejavu brought me all the way back to June 2nd 1970. I realized when I got home that Marina must have asked my uncles and aunties to come over and wait for my father's return to calm him down and perhaps, tame his immediate reaction when he sees the mangled VW. My uncles and aunties knew my father well and were afraid for my life and sensed drama and violence would most likely ensue. I can't say I was relieved and felt safe, in fact I was even more embarrassed and my plan to deal with my father on my own was now just an empty wish and felt like Marina shouldn't have call our relatives to rescue me. When I walked inside the house, uncle Joao Faria who is someone my father respected and was my mother's older brother came to my side and gave me a hug which I would never forget.

"Listen kiddo, it's just a car and the important thing is that nobody is hurt, nobody died, and I can help your father fix it, no sweat." Uncle Joao said.

He too was a cab driver and just like my father had many friends and acquaintances in the auto body/mechanic shop business, including my God Father whom I never had any contact with and who also owned an auto body shop a few miles north up town.

Aunty Rosa was also there, the alcoholic aunt who spent most of her days numb by a good bottle of cachaça to subdue her own pain of having to deal with Marcelo, her adopted and only son who is mentally disabled and requires 24/7 care.

Aunt Joanna was there too, my mother's older sister, who had taken us in when we came back from the Amazon Forest and helped us and fed us through very difficult times. This woman has so much faith in God and her prayers were so beautiful that I believed in God because of her. She would read a bible passage every night for us and pray with us when we were kids and had the occasion sleep overs when my father went on working trips after my mother died. She had and still has a very difficult life with five kids of her own and an adopted one she found in a bus abandoned by his mother as a baby. She's a saint and the devil combined with her beautiful loving ways and constant gossiping habits, but I love her. She was there, praying for me and telling everyone that God would know what to do when my father finally gets home.

"Let's put it in the hands of the lord and surrender to his desires and he will lead Zeze to good understanding and shower him with forgiveness, love and serene thoughts. The divine love is stronger than any evil surrounding our souls." She would repeat.

"Do this people really know my father?" I said to Marina. There ain't no God who will stop that man...no fucking way!

Uncle Pedro, my mother's oldest brother and a religious man himself with auntie Nair were also there, they were the voice of reason and the most respected elders in my family. Uncle Pedro was one of the better off ones and I don't remember what he did for a living, but auntie Nair was the school principal who spanked me with the ruler when I was just five years old. I wasn't very confident her presence there was going to be helpful to me but at that juncture, who the fuck cared? There were so many folks that came to my rescue that I wasn't thinking straight anyways or perhaps they simply came to see the drama up close, watch the great soap opera and have enough material for their own entertainment because it would be an epic scene and a topic of many gossips during the weekend birthday parties for months to come, or till the next dramatic event happens in our chaotic household again.

My father was taking longer than usual to arrive back and some of these folks were starting to leave because they had Sunday supper to tend to with their own children and work the next day which most of them started before sun rise with their journeys to wherever jobs they held at various areas in town.

My anxiety was growing and the air becoming so stuffy that I could barely breathe anymore.

I went into the piano room which we called it Sala de Visita (guest room) and laid down in the small old sofa we had there. In fact, I don't think it was a sofa but rather an old small mattress, which my sister Marina put there to serve as a couch while her students would wait for their piano lessons. She covered it with a nice handmade quilt sawn together with left over scraps by auntie Joana who was quite talented with her old Singer sewing machine. I laid there facing down with my head and feet hanging outside the small mattress. I was looking down the parquet flooring zig zag pattern which puzzled me my entire life and I guess I just tuned off all the noise and chatter in the adjacent room which was still filled with relatives waiting for the freak circus show to start.

Some of the parquet tiles were loose and I could lift them up and see all the dust and other debris stuck underneath the tiles. I would often wonder how much abuse those parquet flooring tiles have endured in that house, how much they have heard and suffered with all the chemicals used to keep them clean and shining on the surface but filthy and dirty in the bottom, almost like the way our family was. We were just like that, with shinning and good manners on the surface but filthy and dirty in the inside, with so much pain and so much trauma from my mother's death at such an early age, with all those motherless and fatherless children, with all the fights, the furniture throwing, guava tree branch and electric chord whooping, blood splashing and name calling…no wonder all this people came to my rescue, they knew that this could be a life or death type of situation with my father, especially when coming back from his fishing trip where he and his fishing buddy Joao Raimundo would drink an entire bottle of 51 cachaça and God only knows what kind of mood my dad would be in…and I had been in those fishing trips and I knew how much he drank and I understood the graveness of the situation very clearly.

My father loved to drink his pinga (which is another name we give it to that liquor in my neck of the wood) and when he went fishing, he would, along with Joao Raimundo who also loved his sugar cane liquor, drink a whole bottle before they come home on Sunday evenings. I think everyone was afraid of what he could do to me and to anyone else who'd be crazy enough to get in the middle of his rages. I for one; I wanted everyone to leave and let me be alone and deal with King Zeze on my own, fight him perhaps, hold on to that electric cord or his belt or the guava branch and if not able to stop him, perhaps inflict the same pain on him, the same pain I was accustomed to see him inflicting on me and my sisters and my mother on a regular basis. I don't care how much tougher those awful moments made us what we are today, that's just not good parenting and I would never do that to my children. I am very sensitive to acts of violence and as much as I love watching movies, I never watch violent ones unless is Pulp Fiction or a Quentin Tarantino flick.

All these thoughts were flowing thru my mind, and I think I felt asleep because I don't remember when my father came home. All I remembered was that I heard a commotion in the other room which was divided by a cream queen size bed sheet as a curtain, and I thought I was having a dream of my brother Cesar gloating about all the fish they had caught and everyone one was in awe about the filled to the brim fish basket he was carrying showing their high prize catches and our food for the next few days.

That's when I heard my father's heavy steps through the front porch, almost like he was running towards the front door. I am sure he saw all the cars in front of the house and thought something very serious must have happened, perhaps someone died, and they were there to break the news to him.

Well, it wasn't too far-fetched for him to think about death when he saw all those cars outside and folks inside the house, the last time we had that many visitors all at once was when my mother had passed away and I am sure that's what popped into his mind; somebody must've died!!!

Perhaps I was already dead and didn't know it, Perhaps I was going to die and was enjoying my last few breaths and regretting not finishing the fucking expensive and yummy banana split ice cream cousin Miriam bought for me. Also, that parquet flooring pattern messed with my intellect and all the analogies I was making about living or dying and what it all meant.

"Who the fuck cares?" I thought. Let's get it over with this drama and move onto the next one, which is inevitable around here. After all, that's what we are really good at in this family; fucking dramas.

My dad opened the front door, which was closed and as usual, stuck on the bottom due to the humidity as the wood expanded on wet days and I remember thinking;

"Why did the close the door with so many people inside such a small house and in a tight room which didn't even have enough seats for everyone?" Maybe they were afraid I was going to run away, I don't know.

He walked inside and immediately started to scream.

"What happened, why are you all here and where is Lenox?" He asked.

The bed sheet curtain to the guest room was closed and he couldn't see me laying there. I was completely unaware if I was having a nightmare or if that was actually happening. I guess I wanted to be a nightmare I could wake up from, but the anticipation of an event sometimes can be much bigger and worse than the event itself. I wasn't dreaming anymore, he's here and he's drunk and scared shitless that something bad might've happened to me, why else would he asked about me? He didn't ask about anybody else. None of those were good signs. That made me even more scared.

Uncle Pedro calmed him down, ask him to go outside with him, which uncle Joao and antie Joana also joined in and walked outside to the front porch which would lead to the garage. I couldn't hear what they told him, but I heard my father screaming a few minutes later and heard his running towards the inside again screaming and yelling:

"Aonde esta esse desgracado? Que diabos eu vou ter que fazer pra ensinar esse infeliz uma licao que ele nunca mais vai esquecer? Where is this disgraceful and problematic child? What the hell do I have to do to teach him a lesson he will never forget for the rest of his life?" Screamed my father.

The scared shitless kid in me took over and I pretended I was asleep and didn't make a move. All I could do was pray for auntie Joana's God to protect me and not let him hit me because I wasn't about to take that shit anymore. I didn't want to hit him back and especially in front of everyone there, but it was either him or me this time around and if I was going down, I was going to go down swinging even though I knew I had done something terrible and something that was going to put us even more behind financially, not to mention emotionally and mentally for the next few months and years, if not forever tattooed in my body and memory given the graveness of the situation.

My uncles held my father as he walked back into the house almost destroying the front door which got stuck again and he couldn't open with all the force he put on. Nida started to cry and as she held my youngest brother Sandro on her arms, who was still an infant. She then asked the smaller kids Cesar and Sergio to go outside and stay there. My sisters were getting desperate with the begging and getting down on their knees imploring for him not to hit me. I was fucking frozen, almost like waiting for the burning sensation of that clothing steamer iron electric cord to hit my back and my legs as if I was ready and welcoming the warm sensation of the cord slashing my skin and the blood running down my back and my legs. I was also planning my attack however, how to take the first whooping, then throw my first punch and go after his throat. I had no chance however, my old man was strong as an ox.

When you see those things often, it's almost like some sort of desensitizing phenomenon takes over your senses and you welcome that type of abuse, almost like you want it in order to change things around, as if you deserve it for being such an idiot and not know the fucking difference between the brake and the gas pedal, a moron for not being able to see that girl crossing the street on her bike, or even better, anticipate that she would. Or better yet, go fucking fishing and not drive your father's boss car when you are just a kid and don't know how. A failure for not passing your stupid math class on 7th grade and having the stigma and the reputation of being ugly, unwanted, stupid and a complete loser…that's how I felt, and my father never helped me feel any different. He didn't know how and that's probably how he felt about me too.

But I wasn't all those things, I was doing well in school now, was going to a great school and nobody had to pay for it. I was playing basketball with the best players around and feeling confident and growing up. I had a job, was independent, and a fighter. I simply didn't have good luck in some of my adventures and I am sure just about everyone has similar stories about their teenage years and dealing with their parents I am assuming. The mind is a strange and mysterious thing however and it fucks with you often if you let it but sometimes, we don't know how to stop it so…that's how I felt; like an idiot and a loser and someone who deserved the hand life was dealing to me.

He moved the curtain with such violence everything came down into pieces, he walked inside the room where I was, and he called my name for the entire neighborhood to hear it. I didn't move, I don't think I was even breathing at that point. All I could think, and feel was the pain in my skin and in my flesh, nothing else. I felt the heat of whatever apparatus he was going to use on my skinny body and I was already bleeding even before he laid his hands or his torturing gadgets on me.

I was cursing my mother again for having more children after the doctors told her not to have any more kids. She could have stopped at Marta's and not keeping on trying to have a boy. I was mad at her for not having her own voice, good health and a sense of compassion and saying no to all the unjustifiable violence and abuse for things that didn't matter much at all, but those events marked us forever and made us who we are today...FUCK!!!

I was disappointed at her for not dying sooner, she could have died before she gave birth to me so none of this senseless bullshit would be happening. I was furious at auntie Joana's God for not protecting me from all this wrath of a life and disgusted with the prospects because I was only 14 years old...and hopeless.

My father called me again, screaming:

"Lenox, wake up, get the fuck up and look at me."

His voice was trembling, he was crying, and I haven't seen my father cry often, if ever.

I turned around and felt my entire body and my eyes filled with fear, desperation, disappointment, horror, and everything a kid shouldn't be experiencing.

I turned to him and unleashed:

"Go ahead, just kill me at once, just hit me as hard as you can, just break all my fucking bones, knock all my buck teeth out, draw all the blood from my bonny legs and my skeleton like body, get your belt and all the other torture apparatus you use to soothe your own anger and punish my body and draw blood from me, expose my flesh, just like you do it with everyone else around here, I don't fucking care anymore, I deserve it. Go ahead, I don't give a shit what you do to me anymore, but I am not responsible what I might do to you. I don't care anymore." I said crying and screaming my lungs out.

I was surprisingly firm, clear and collected for a second even though I was red lining, crying and out of control. I didn't need all those people there to protect me anymore. I wasn't sure who that brave and scared screaming kid was, but I stood up for myself and something overcame me and for the first time I could handle my father on my own without an audience or anyone's pity. Perhaps not physically but certainly mentally. I told him what happened and that I was willing to work to pay to fix his boss's car and the neighbor's wall and that I wouldn't do that again. I also told him I wanted to learn how to drive and that's why I didn't go fishing. My father gave me that blue eye stare which I knew what it meant but from that point forward I wasn't afraid anymore.

"We will settle this later when these people are fucking gone." He said walking away.

He also said he would talk to me in the morning and that I was going to pay for everything. I could see the veins on his neck dilating and his deep blue eyes bulging out of the eye sockets which was the sign of his rage and also his fears. He had that fucking scary and intense look which only meant he needed to vent that anger out on somebody, and I was on the menu that night, but he couldn't touch me because there were too many people around, he didn't want witnesses for his transgressions I guess, besides they wouldn't let him. Without a doubt, Marina's thinking on having my relatives there did help because the outcome of that episode would have been very traumatic if there were only us there to share the news with him. It is conceivable that we might have killed each other that night because I was going to defend myself and my sisters from him.

My father made me pay for all the damage and he ended up getting the car as a gift from his boss. We didn't speak or even look at each other's direction for months, he didn't speak to me the next morning either like he said he would, and that accident was never brought up in my household again. That dreadful Sunday evening was never discussed amongst my relatives, at least in front of me during many of the birthday parties or during our fishing camping trips to the Araguaia river every winter where we'd all be together. Part of me died that day, maybe the scared and afraid me was gone and the confident and brave Lenox emerged from the ashes, dirt and dust, perhaps from under the parquet flooring a new me was born. I grew emotionally and mentally and felt stronger after that, and I carried that feeling and courage ever since. Shift happens, and I had made a shift… for better.

CHAPTER XIII
The Pink Panther

I had so many unanswered questions as a young child and the obsession of leaving home and running away consumed my life from the time I'd wake up to the time I go to bed. I would dream while awake about living somewhere else, having a different family and how unfair for me and my siblings to have been brought into this world. When I closed my eyes and fell asleep, I would have nightmares of all kinds, specially about a funky black table with caster wheels on it and a bunch of shiny black shoes slowly walking around it.

The following week after the VW crash, my sisters were trying to get me to do things with them, anything outside the house because I was cooped up in my room staring at the ceiling and silent for days. I didn't want to be a part of anything, the only thing in my mind was planning how to become independent, how to leave and make a new path on my own, a new life away from all the madness at home. I started to plan how to escape that circus and what could be the consequences of such an ambitious endeavor.

My sisters used to get their hair done near my aunt Justina's house just a few blocks from where we lived. The place was small with only three chairs, one for hair, one for manicure and pedicure and the other was this helmet looking apparatus thing which I had no idea what it was for. Occasionally, my sister Moema helped out her friend and owner Teresa, with manicure and pedicure on weekends when the demand was high and in exchange my sisters got their hair and nails done for free.

Teresa who was this nice middle-aged woman who had been married 4 times already. Each time was because the previous husband had died of some strange disease and unknown causes. Sometimes I sat there and waited for my sisters to finish whatever they were doing, and I would listen to their conversation and would always wonder if those stories were real or if Teresa was full of shit because how can you have 4 husbands and they all died? I didn't buy that and in my mind she was the problem I thought.

"She is killing these men and taking their money or something like that because that's ought to be a world record to lose four husbands to death and she wasn't even that old." I thought.

Teresa didn't have the most attractive face, but she had a killer, beautiful, curvy and voluptuous body which I could understand why so many men wanted to marry her, she was definitely very sexy and extremely flirty. I on the other hand was starting to discover sex and feeling these different feelings in my funky body so Teresa was someone who would make an appearance in my fantasies under the blankets after those James Bond movies I used to watch with my father late at night. James Bond movies have a special meaning with my discovering of sexuality and my appreciation for beautiful women, thru 007 I discovered masturbation.

I wasn't speaking to my father at all, and I needed to get a haircut because the lads were picking on me at school due to the afro that was getting out of control, and it made me look even skinnier because of my height and the extreme out of proportion length of my limbs and my bamboo like built. Since father and I weren't on speaking terms, I approached my sister Marina and asked if she had any money that I could use to get my hair trimmed and she said she didn't have any, however, she could talk to Teresa and ask her to cut my hair for free since Moema had worked there recently to help Teresa out and she could probably find a slot for me during the week. I immediately said yes, I wanted to see Teresa up close and wouldn't mind at all going to a women's place to get my hair cut, after all Teresa was way better looking than Antonio, the psycho killer looking barber I had gone to my entire life.

I arrived to get my hair cut on a Thursday evening in one of my days off from basketball. There was nobody there except me and Teresa and, from the first glance I had of Teresa, I was aroused and remained as such for the duration and even I left her studio and for quite some time after if you really want to know the truth. I sat on her chair, and I immediately noticed she was wearing a lowcut blouse which showed her cleavage and teased the onlookers with the outer edge of her nipples peeking out of the white bra she was wearing. I never really paid attention to what she was saying or talking about, I was distracted by her sex appeal…and boy was she sexy, and could she yap? She wouldn't shut the fuck up.

I guess one of the pre-requisites of being a hairdresser is that you must have a lot to talk about because without an exception, every single hairdresser I know talks a lot more than I care to listen. Usually the talk is about nothing, about somebody else's life and misery but literately unequivocally about nothing.

Teresa mumbled about something my sister Moema had told her about my hair and I didn't really understand what she was talking about, and I must have just nodded "yes" or something. My mind and my body were both raging with thoughts and reactions to that gorgeous body and the fact she was touching my hair and perhaps murdered four husbands already…wow that's sexy, maybe I will be next, what a way to die I reckoned.

Perhaps all her ex-husbands died of a heart attack while having wild sex with Teresa. I don't know about other man but in my mind some women just have that "wild, sex, pleasure" thing written on their forehead and it's hard to get away from that vibe they put out, you men out there know exactly what I mean, and I do not mean as a bad thing at all, I guess that's what we call having sex appeal. Whatever it was, Teresa had it and I'd been completely engulfed in it and didn't want my experience to end.

"Who gives a fuck about my hair? Just do whatever you want Teresa but do it slowly please." I was talking to myself still without a clue about what she was mumbling and I agreeing about just a few minutes ago.

Truth be told, I got a bit concerned about the strong smell of some of the stuff she was applying to my hair. I was used to get in and get out in 20 minutes with my father's barber and not even look in the mirror because regardless of what Antonio the serial psycho killer barber would do, he wasn't any fun to be looking at and I always looked the fucking same, dog shit ugly if you ask me or anybody who remembers it.

Teresa put some white paste on my hair, wrapped with a plastic film and brought this machine that I needed to put my head inside for the product to take effect, I think it's a called a drier. I complied as requested and since she was so nice to me, I was being as cooperative as I could. Inside that funky hot alien looking helmet type of machine, I stayed for a good 15-20 minutes and fell asleep thinking about Teresa and how she murdered each of her four husbands.

"Did she use the same method with all of them? Does she have a killer who does it for her and have wild sex with her after they kill their pray? Does she strangle them while on top of them?" I dozed off with a thousand thoughts of how she would kill me. Perhaps she'd take me to the back room and took my virginity away. It wouldn't be a bad way to die really, I thought.

I have been on a verge of being killed couple of times in my young life (at least in my mind) and from now on, anytime that threat of being killed is eminent, I will try to get an appointment with Teresa and if I have to get zapped, I want to go under Teresa's watch, whatever she does, whatever her men were getting when they expired, that's what I'm having.

I felt a tap on my shoulder, and I woke up awkwardly and drooling only to see Teresa with a napkin on her hands telling me to clean the drool from my face and that she needed to take me out of the space helmet type oven I was under for the last 30 minutes. I was in a daze as if I died and came back and had wild sex with Teresa along the way. She removed me from under the machine as I cleaned my face from that distinct smell of hot drool that wetted my t-shirt and her chair as well. Teresa gave me some instructions on how to take care of my hair for the next few days and I said "ok, tudo bem," and whatever else I needed to say to get out of that funk smell of rotten eggs emanating from my hair. She takes the plastic film off my head, and I noticed my hair was straight. I mean straight to the point I looked like a porcupine.

"Did you cut my hair? What is this? I look like a porcupine Teresa, what did you fucking do?" I asked in complete confusion.

Teresa: "I did what your sister asked me to do, I relaxed your curls and straighten your hair because Moema said you didn't like your afro look, so I straighten it."

"What the fuck Teresa, I didn't ask you to straighten my hair, did I?" I replied very upset.

"I asked you when you sat down and you said it was fine, were you listening?" Said Teresa with a surprised look on her face as if I had given her my consent.

I realized I wasn't paying attention to anything she said earlier. How could I? I was distracted by her cleavage and the C cup breasts size, the four dead husbands and the hormones raging inside my body all trying to talk at the same time…how could I hear anything?

I ran out of there as fast as I could and when I got home, I noticed my brother-in-law Cleone's V8, blue Ford Maverick parked in front of our house. Cleone was this real good-looking guy who's been a playboy all his life, had the nicest cars, smelled like a fucking chimenea from all the Carlton cigs he smoked, and had this full head of free-flowing beautiful hair that I'd gotten tired of hearing my sisters talking about it. He was Marina's boyfriend then and is her husband now…he still smokes like a motherfucker, already had two strokes, a stint put in his heart and his lungs are completely blackened and fucked. He's completely depressed, suffers from panic attacks, drives my sister Marina crazy but he won't quit his Carltons, no sir…just like she won't quit him and dump his ass.

Before I went inside the house, I put my head under the garden faucet and ran water on my head and rubbed my hands on it back and forth for a long time with the hopes I could just wash that shit away. I rubbed it front to back, side to side under the water as hard as I could with hopes that the rotten egg smelling shit was going to be washed off and my hair was going to go back to being curly and kinky again. I guess you don't know what you have till you lose it. I didn't have a mirror to look into, so to avoid any teasing from my brother-in-law I took my shirt off, wrapped it onto my head and walked inside our home without saying anything to anyone, went straight into the shower and started to wash my new look away. I used half of a shampoo bottle that my stepmother used to leave on the window base and another half bottle of a really thick conditioner called Neutrox which was this nasty yellow butter like thing my sister Tata used on her hair which was as kinky as mine except longer and better taken cared of. That crap Tata put on her hair was lethal, it would make my hair curly and soft but with the curls and softness came the dandruff which we had so much of it that I actually believed we could fry those dandruff flakes and eat them as potato chips and not be as hungry as I was in so many occasions.

Low and behold, 30 minutes under the shower and I thought I removed the hair product Teresa put on my hair and I felt good about it. Once I get out from under the shower and I looked in the mirror, I couldn't believe my own eyes, it was worse and now it just looked like the porcupine had put some butter on its pines and the pines were a bit softer but still pointing up and I could not have looked any worst, if that was a real possibility!

I went to bed that night with one thought in mind:

"How the hell am I going to go to school looking this hideous tomorrow? Should I wear a hat? Shit, they don't allow students to wear hats. What if I shave my head? Who would shave it for me? I don't own clippers and I have no money to get it cut or shaved…fuck!"

Thoughts were running wild in my head. I would need to go to the barber shop and ask him to do it but, I didn't have any money to do that. I couldn't sleep because whatever plan I came up with, it would be tough to pull it off because my father wasn't speaking to me due to the car accident, my sisters didn't have any money, I can't wear a hat in school, what am I supposed to do? I decided I was going to own it and walk to school next day as if nothing had happened. Except that people were going to make fun of me and my chance with girls which was then close to zero, has now been downgraded to below zero.

Next morning, I woke up earlier than normal and went to take a long shower to see If I could wash some of that porcupine look away from my hair. Again, I used up all the shampoo available and all the conditioner I could put my hands on. It didn't work, the curl relaxer was way too strong and only time will solve this, but I don't have time. I thought perhaps I get to school very early and take my seat in the back of the room as usual and just stay there all day till I had to go home. That didn't work either because in the middle of our first class, I needed to go to the bathroom badly. I am a morning person and so are my intestines which are very regular and works on its own morning schedule religiously. So, I collected all the courage I could, got up and walked out of the classroom as fast as I could and went to the restroom. Well, there's really no problem there because everyone had their back to me and since I was seating behind everyone else, in the back of the classroom, nobody paid attention to my exit. I spent most of my time in the bathroom planning on how to get back to the classroom without being completely humiliated by those fuckers who love to laugh at my expense for any little thing. I looked in the mirror a dozen times and wetted my hair, moved it to one side and another but nothing made that porcupine look disappear, no sir! I considered going home from that bathroom and not returning to class…ever, but I needed to get my things in the classroom. I considered never coming back to school again but that was too dramatic, and I knew this would pass and my hair would eventually grow kinky again. That's when I realized that I liked my kinky hair, that I missed my tight curls, and I hated my sisters for putting me through that fucking curl relaxer experience.

Unbeknownst to me, upon my return to the classroom, everyone had already noticed my new hair style and when I came back, the moment I opened the classroom door on the bottom of the stairs and started the long and very reluctant walk to my seat in the back of the classroom, my classmates were whistling Henry Mancini's Pink Panther song and the fucking joke caught on like a motherfucker wildfire, thru the entire school. I thank God for the inexistence of any devices, YouTube or social media those days, otherwise I'd gone viral for all the wrong reasons and I don't believe I would have survived the embarrassment. I walked all the way to my seat, grabbed my stuff and stayed away from school for about two weeks. Yes, the embarrassment was too great to bear and I was willing to risk getting spanked by my father than to give those motheruckers at Colegio Objetivo any more reason to poke fun at my ridiculous existence.

I would leave home as if I was going to school and instead, walk around city parks, visit a few music stores, go to libraries, and stop at any live music taking place around city corners. I'd come home, eat lunch and head to work and practice afterwards. At work it wasn't that big of a deal because I could wear a hat, and nobody really noticed anything but at practice things got a bit dicey. My teammates weren't as brutal but they noticed and poked fun at me but because I was becoming a popular player and respected by my peers, the coaches put an end to the jokes right from the beginning and I was able to wear a head band and carry on with basketball as usual.

After the first week of skipping school, my sister Tata picked up a telephone call from Colegio Objetivo staff asking why I hadn't been to school for the last week or so. When I came home that night, my sister called me into the girls' bedroom and asked me if I was going to school. I told her that I wasn't because I was too embarrassed of my hair and that people were singing and whistling the Pink Panther song when I walked into the classroom and around school and I couldn't bare the embarrassment. She started to laugh uncontrollably and said that she needed to tell our father about it because if he found out the consequences could be dire, and she was going to pay the price for it as well for not telling him.

"Please don't say anything to dad, he will beat me up and I can't handle that shit anymore. I beg you and if you don't say anything I'll do your chores for two weeks straight." I appealed and negotiated myself out of trouble as I knew she hated doing her chores.

"Agreed." Tata replied while still laughing uncontrollably. "Pink Panther? That's good shit Lenox!" She said giggling and happy she didn't have to do chores for a while.

What a sister right?

A few days later I received my paycheck from the typewriting job I had which wasn't much, and I needed to pay to fix my father boss's car as agreed and buy socks because I couldn't wear my father's socks anymore due to our spat and we weren't on speaking terms, so going into his bedroom to get his socks like I had done for years was completely out of the question. So, I took my paycheck and walked into the barber shop and asked him if he could cut my hair as low as possible without having to shave my head. He said he could and that my hair was going to be very short, but it was already growing underneath that hideous pink panther mane.

Psycho Killer Antonio:

"This shit looks nasty man; how did you get yourself in this type of predicament?" He was laughing out loud and telling his other customers what happened to me once I told him the story.

That night, I heard my father asking my stepmother Nida in the kitchen why my hair was so short and what had happened to me. She said I didn't like the hair style the hairdresser had given me and that I went to his barber shop and asked him to cut my hair as short as he could without shaving my head.

"Good, because he looked like that cartoon they are always watching on tv, A Pantera Cor de Rosa." He said while giggling and I couldn't believe he said that because I never talked to him about the nick name I was given in school and this fucking guy was poking fun of my due too… what the fuck!

I guess my father wasn't too off based on certain things and for sure in agreement with my classmates. Well, I learned my lesson: Don't trust any hairdresser specially if she's hot and don't lose your focus from the task at hand when you see a beautiful woman, she will literally fuck you.

CHAPTER XIV
Teaching an Old Dog a New Trick

"Que a arte de viver seja o seu primeiro projeto, e que o seu primeiro projeto seja de viver com arte."

"That the art of living be your first project, and that your first project is to live with art."

This was what I wrote to my sister Tata on the cover of a LP album by Djavan, one of her favorite artists, which I bought at a pawn shop as a gift when she entered Architecture school in January of 1980 when I was 15 years old.

Life was getting interesting. I started to save some money from the typewriting job which I received a small raise for good performance. It was mango season and our mango tree produced so many mangos that I couldn't keep up with all the sweet yellow and red fruits getting ripe all at once. My customers liked them not bruised and I enjoyed picking them by hand. I often climbed that tall mango tree and maneuvered my skinny body like a monkey thru its thick and thin limbs to get the mangoes before they fell and got bruised or were eaten by the many resident birds. I had my customer base at the schools nearby and neighbors who would buy as many as I brought to them, and the challenge was finding time to climb the tree to pick the mangos before they fall and get bruised. The neighbors I could take care of during the weekend when I didn't have to go to school or work. Although I had games on weekends which made things challenging at times, but my games were usually at night and that left me plenty of time for my shoe polishing business and the mango delivering enterprise around the neighborhood. I needed to find a way to sell more mangos at the school recess though. I went down the family tree and recruited the only unemployed soldier I could find; my 10-year-old brother Cesar. I prepared the mangos and he'd bring the basket filled with beautiful fresh sweet mangos to the schools nearby and sell them in exchange for a huge 10% cut which he had no clue how much that was. However, he learned fast that he could make money and buy candies from the convenience store across the street from our house, specifically, the sweet popcorn in the pink bag with the diamonds and aqua marines and all the beautiful fake semi-precious stones in the bottle of the bag.

Life and business were thriving, I was busy at school and doing well, busy at work and being very productive by making my boss/auntie Justina happy and very popular with everyone else with my good work that reflected well on her. I was getting better and better in basketball, selling plenty of mangos with my new ten-year-old salesman. My father was coming around and was now talking to me again and even offered to teach me how to drive on this old blue sky color VW Passat he was able to scrounge from aunt Cro after the accident with the VW TL. I guess things turned out pretty good after all, but the process wasn't all that smooth...when is it ever?

I had always wanted to see the ocean for the first time and dreamt about tasting the salty water to see if it was salty for real...I never believed it was. My sister Tata was dating a boy named Carlos in the city of Brasilia, the Brasilian capital which is about 200 kilometers from Goiania. He was nice and very attentive the two times I had met him at some of the functions I used to attend with my sister at PUC University where she was studying Architecture. Carlos had a brother named Deidinho who lived in Rio de Janeiro and had invited Tata to spend a weekend at his apartment in Niteroi which was just across the Guanabara Bay and 13 kilometers over the ocean Rio/Niteroi bridge. These two boys were cousins of my brother-in-law Cleone, and my father, believe it or not, liked them even though I don't think he knew that Tata was dating Carlos. So, I invited myself to go with her when she told me she was going to Rio de Janeiro and to my surprise she said yes. She said I would need to pay for my bus ticket because she only had money for hers and she couldn't help me. I said that I could do that, and I had saved enough to buy a bus ticket. I hoped my father wouldn't create a problem for me to join her and go see the ocean and its allegedly salt water for the first time. I was supper excited and couldn't sleep or eat with the anticipation of jumping in the ocean and swim thru those waves I could only see on television. "What, me in the ocean, in Rio de Janeiro?" I was in disbelief and in my mind, already there.

I asked my stepmother to talk to my father for me and reminded her that I was doing well in school, I had a job, I practice every day, I took care of my brother Cesar and even helped him make money to help with clothes and shoes, and I always did my (and Tata's) chores around the house without any problems and without having to be reminded of. And most importantly, I have not gotten into trouble for months. She agreed to talk to my father but asked me to understand if he said no because my father always said "no" to anything we'd ask him, no matter what it was.

"I can ask him for you to go but he'll most likely say no and when he does, can you promise me you won't cause problems so there's no drama? It's been nice and quiet here the last few months, don't you think?" Nida asked me with her soft and angelical voice, which was impossible not to agree with her, even if I didn't mean it.

"No, I'm going to get on that bus regardless and I might never come back, you can tell him that too." I walked away towards the front door with an attitude that could only bring more problems only to return and add:

"Why does everything around here have to be so difficult and has to be father's idea? Why does he exercise so much control over everyone even if it doesn't cost him anything? I am fifteen years old, and I work since I was thirteen, I am doing well in school, a private school nobody pays for it, I do my chores and I contribute, we all do. Why can't I go on a small trip and see the ocean which I dream of doing so? Oh yes, by the way…with my own money? What else do I need to do to earn the right to have a little fun?" I started to question everything, not to my father obviously, I was inquisitive but not oblivious or ignorant about who the boss, the master, the king was.

Nida was one of those sweet, calm, and collected type of people. She was exactly what was needed in our household, but I felt sorry for her. I felt sorry because she was verbally, mentally, emotionally, and sometimes physically abused by my father who was so dominating that he didn't leave any room for anybody else to breathe in his presence and we could all sense that Nida was running out of air and being suffocated in that toxic environment. She loved him and he loved her, no doubt about that, go figure…but living with my father was just tense, complicated, fearful, stressful, bat shit crazy and flat-out breath taking for all the wrong reasons.

I gave Tata the money to buy my bus ticket to Rio de Janeiro before I had the consent of my father. I thought that if I put the energy that he was going to say "yes," and believed that I was going to be able to go without any problems, perhaps he would say yes and if he didn't, I would have to go thru with it anyways because I never like to make threats or say something I wouldn't do. I am going and that's the end of that, up to him to play along with it and let me see the ocean for the first time, twenty plus fucking hours away in a cramped, stinky National Expresso bus.

I have always believed that a man's word is more important than any contract and any signature on a piece of paper and I have lived my entire life under those premises. If I say I am going to do something, I do it, no fucking excuses!!!

"I am going to Rio de Janeiro even if I never have to return to this place again." I told Tata and she obliged.

To my surprise, and I don't know what my father really said but Nida told me the next day that I could go, and that King Zeze wasn't too happy with it, but she had made a deal with him which she didn't share with me what it was. Perhaps she promised him more sex, I don't know but I never really cared to ask except, I thanked her and gave her a huge kiss on her forehead and told her I was going to bring her a gift from Rio, a place she had never been either, for she too had never seen the ocean even though she was already in her forties.

Goiania is over 1000 miles from Rio de Janeiro and the bus trip was over 20 hours in a cramped and packed 42 passenger bus without air conditioner, with a bunch of stops and plenty of opening and closing the little window to let air in when someone would use the miniscule bathroom which was right next to our seats 41A and 41B all the way in the back of the National Expresso Company bus.

I didn't find any of that very challenging or even difficult and the smell coming from the bathroom wasn't much different than the one I was used to in many of the locker rooms and schools I have been in my life to that point. Or the one in my house where eight children and two adults had to share the same bathroom. If I open the window, I couldn't smell anything, and the fresh air would make the trip pleasant, and the excitement was building after every kilometer we covered and the many stops we made along the way. My sister and I would buy one "café com leite" (latte) and share a piece of peach pie she made for the road and brought it in her handbag wrapped in aluminum foil. It was delicious and she was baking these beautiful pies to sell them and using either low sugar or no sugar at all which I thought it was strange.

"That's weird, why won't you use sugar?" I asked her surprised after she mentioned she was using dates as sweeteners instead of sugar because we used sugar for everything.

"Sugar isn't very healthy for our teeth and it's addictive." Tata replied with confidence.

I never heard such thing before and I thought she was nuts and somewhat too forward thinking, but I couldn't argue with how yummy her pies were.

"You should open a bakery and sell these pies to more people, they are so yummy and tasty, soft and moist, and yet, according to you healthy and sugar free." I said half-jokingly but still confident my sister was too modern and liberal with her thinking.

"I'm selling pies to pay for college in architecture school, I want to be an architect but don't want to bake pies for a living." Replied Tata with the certainty of a twenty-year-old, and for Brazilian standards already a full fletched adult.

My sisters had very big dreams in life as well. Marina had just entered medical school in her first try and to everyone's surprise. Medical school is very competitive in Brazil that only the well to do or super smart kids get to pass the vigorous and sometimes corrupted entry examinations. I say only the very rich because the private high schools and prep schools cost a lot of money and we never had money to attend those institutions and get a leg up on the competition. I was the only one in my family going to a private school but only because of basketball. Those types of private schools were so distant from our reality, and they were for the privileged, rich and well-connected kids, not us.

That year there were 110 open spots for medical school entrance in Goiania's federal university and thousands of applicants for the entry test which were comprised of essay answers, difficult and very competitive of course with only 110 of the highest grades receiving an accepting letter for one of those spots. During the announcement of the results, we were all anxious and nervous because if Marina didn't get in, it would be very tense in our house due to my father's unrealistic expectations which today I see how crazy and unrealistic he was and how much he pushed us to get more out of school and life than he ever did as a high school dropout. I see my father as someone who thought and saw more in us than we ever thought and saw in ourselves even though he didn't know how to communicate that to us. With the exception of my old man, who was at work that day, we all went to my aunt Justina's house to hear the results on the radio which was announced from 1st place all the way to 110th place in order of test results and not alphabetical order with the highest grade being announced first. It didn't really matter what placed your name was called as long as your name was announced. Everyone went to the same medical school, and it was more a matter of prestige and bragging rights to be top ten of the class. We just wanted to hear her name being called on the tiny Phillips radio seating on top of the glass coffee table in the middle of the living room and everyone seating around it listening to every name being called and every now and then there would be someone we knew being announced and we celebrated as if Brazil had scored a gol against Italy in the world cup.

Our hopes were running empty, the mood was flat, and we were all pretty sad already for there were only two spots left and Marina's name hadn't been called. Marina had studied so much, she sacrificed her entire teenage years teaching piano lessons, making hangers and taking care of us and for her not to get in, it will be devastating, very concerning and scary due to my father's reaction.

"Shit, my father isn't going to take this well. He expects her to get in and this could be a major setback in the small progress we've made in the last months and years." I thought to myself as we were all saying our silent prayers and hoping that God stepped up to the plate and showed up when it mattered the most.

"In 109th place, Marina Gomes Jube…" The announcer called her name.

"Holy shit, sweet Jesus, is this really happening? We will have a doctor in our family." I yelled in complete disbelief as I had already accepted she hadn't been called and chaos was about to ensue at home.

We all jumped for joy on top of each other crying and kissing everyone and everything in front of us and celebrated as if our futebol national team had scored a winning goal in the finals of the world cup against our archrivals Argentina. One of the happiest moments of our lives for sure and one we'll never forget. My father was so proud of her, and Marina became our family pride and joy that day, a doctor in the family of really poor people whose parents never stepped a single foot in any college campus, whose father never even went to high school…not even to sell peach pies, decorated hangers or mangos during recess.

Couple of years later was Moema's and Tata's turn and they both took the test to enter Dental school which was just as competitive but not as popular or perhaps as prestigious as medical school. After two tries, the first at Goiania Federal University and another a week later at Anapolis Federal University just 50 kilometers from our hometown they didn't get in and for not getting in, they were spanked, ridiculed and embarrassed by my father who told them they weren't good enough for anything, that they should go find a husband to take care of them because they were incapable in getting into a much easier Dental school.

We didn't know how to react to his comments and how to reconcile such ignorance and make any sense of his unrealistic, mean, sexist, discriminating and abusive words. Did I mention they got spanked and beaten for failing?

We knew it was going to be nasty if they didn't pass it and we feared for the worst. I honestly don't know how we didn't turn into drug addicts and completely fucked up people from hearing and living such terrible moments in crucial rites of passages in life such as simply just trying to get into college. I can't comprehend how we didn't turn out like a bunch of losers, without any self-esteem and healthy encouragement.

My two sisters were fucking hard working young women who lacked everything a person can lack: enough food, good clothing, shoes, socks, a space to grow as a woman, a mother, they lacked love and affection and yet they worked so hard, they sacrificed so much only to be told they're worthless pieces of shit by their own father and on top of that they were beaten and spanked for failing a very difficult exam which required an absurd amount of work and luck to pass. Did I mention they were grown women already? They were receiving my father's worst treatment and were demoralized for not being able to get into dental school. They studied hard and worked extra hours to making extra money to pay for prep school, but neither one of them got into dental school even the following year. I believe it wasn't their calling and they were doing what they were told to do and what they perceived as their obligation to pass those difficult tests and set the world on fire with their new careers once they finished college. It wasn't meant to be.

Tata decided to follow her heart and I believe that was more because of the lifestyle and the people she perceived to be in architecture school than the profession itself and she got into a private university which had a lot less competition because it was private, and it wasn't in the health field like medicine and dentistry which were careers perceived to be well respected and well paid.

So, Tata's choice was to beg my father's rich boss and her God Father Olavo Pires to help her pay for college which he agreed to it but the process of getting the portion of tuition money monthly was always embarrassing and tedious because Olavo Pires was not a man one could trust. He didn't mean what he said, and he often didn't finish what he started so it was embarrassing for all of us and felt like begging for Tata and my father who worked for the idiot for many years and felt indebted to him for helping Tata pay for college.

We were poor but trying to move up the social economic ladder, so pride and ego weren't part of our vocabulary and played no role in our decisions. Begging and leaving our pride and self-esteem in the gutter to move ahead in the world were part of the equation and we never felt we were weak for doing that.

"Fuck it, we beg if we have to and if it hurts, oh well, we are familiar with pain and it's only temporary." We would say to each other when we had to go ask Olavo for the tuition money.

That ritual of going to Olavo Pires office or his house to ask for the promised portion of the tuition money became a common place and one I experienced with Tata many times as I accompanied her in plenty of her trips to the Olavo's home or office. I also accompanied her to the awesome parties with the hip and cool classmates of hers at PUC Architecture School in Goiania, many of whom were homosexuals, artists, and extremely creative people.

The parties were so much fun, and because I have always been oblivious to drugs and alcohol, still am to this day, which was a constant amongst that group of very creative minds, their events were filled with joy and it triggered my curiosity for arts, for writing, for theatre and music. I enjoyed their clothing, the fact that they were hip and out of the box so to speak, and they actually talked to me regardless of my age, how skinny I was or how many zits I had on my face didn't' matter to them. I felt I had found my crowd which was much older than me, but they embraced and accepted my weirdness without prejudice which it wasn't commonplace.

They were non-judgmental and introduced me to great music and great theatre which I enjoy to this day. Artists like Talking Heads, Queen, David Bowie, Super Tramp and so many others. I started to appreciate arts through my new older friends, and I am forever thankful to all of them for the constant curiosity and open-mindedness they instilled and inspired me with. Sure, I wasn't fully aware of their sexuality and at first found myself feeling a bit awkward when I'd see two men kissing or two girls making out in the middle of a party, but I soon realized they were just being free, experimenting with theirs senses and their desires. Plenty of Tata's friends would come to our house and a phenomenon would take place: My father treated them extremely nice, courteously and a lot better than he treated us.

He was sweet and open and welcoming to all of Tata's gay friends and even though only my brother Sergio had homosexual inclination which my father detested, he treated Tata's friends with so much respect and kindness that we were all pleased and very impressed not to mention extremely confused and surprised. Sergio didn't get the same treatment and that only showed me that my father probably just didn't like his kids perhaps because he treated everyone nice, except us and that hurt more than swallowing our pride and asking Olavo Pires for money to pay for college tuition for Tata.

We were always very scared to bring friends home because he treated us so badly at times that we didn't want our friends to see that and for the fear they'd be treated with the same contempt. He didn't and having friends over became a habitual thing we all learned to practice because it took the edge off and released some of the tension and pressure for us and made our lives easier around the house.

Tata was very involved in various projects at the university, specially the one called "Via Lactea." Which, to this day was one of the best comedy skits I have been to, and I have been to a lot of them. Via Lactea was a theatre group that started out of Pedro Zorzetti's mind and grew exponentially in Goiania and across the country. They would take current national news and events and turn them into comedy skits with lots of great music which they would also sing and dance to it. It was simply beautiful and very creative. Too bad Pedro Zorzetti died of AIDS a few years back because I heard thru Tata he was putting the crew back together and planning to go back on the road again. It was like Saturday Night Live of sorts except funnier and in theaters across the country.

Moema was also now attending University after passing the entry test (Vestibular) to become a social worker but I think she just wanted to get into any kind of university so she could escape my father's wrath and show him that she was able to attend university and get him off her back. She's the most sensitive of all my siblings, the most loving although it is difficult to say who is the most loving sister I have because they are all so incredibly kind and beautiful women and ever so genuine loving to everyone around them. It's almost as if they wanted to make up for my mother's absence so early in our lives and instead of losing a mother, we gained three others. They still behave that way to this day, they shower us with loving comments each and every time we see them, and they will go to great lengths to make sure we are safe, happy and healthy.

I believe Moema is the strongest of my sisters, but I don't think she knows that. She has this incredible capacity to make a person feel at home and strong any time you speak to her. She makes me feel attractive and vain every time we speak on the phone, mostly on WhatsApp video calls. She's also the most vulnerable and fragile of all my siblings and she always wears her heart literally on her sleeve. It's an intense way to live and she suffers a great deal because of it. She often cries about the simplest things, she's the most sensitive to criticism and the most loving person I have ever met and yet, strength, weakness, sadness, happiness, tears, joy, fear, courage, discipline, self-doubt, low self-esteem, beauty, braveness, and love; these attributes make Moema this incredibly strong human being who is constantly in conflict with her mind and heart. She struggles to live in the present moment and tends to be always missing someone or something when she's having a good time. I understand her challenges, she wants to share all the good things in life with her children, and with the many people she loves and that robs her of the moments she could be having for herself. She is also the most selfless person I know and I am proud to be her brother. It's almost like self-sabotage and it is challenging sometimes to share with her my thoughts because she gets worried and hurt easily and elated at the same time if what I share is something positive.

Moema graduated from university and went to work for a non-profit clinic in her city of Belo Horizonte where she lives with her beautiful family consisting of her husband Alex, and her two kids Janaina and Gabriel. She works for very little money and with minimum resources, but she helps the poor, assists needy families and sick people with so much conviction and love that It brings tears to my eyes and joy to my heart when I write about her. She rides a bus sometimes for almost two hours to get to work daily and has been doing that for over 30 years. I admire her humbleness; I idolize her commitment and envy her strength even though from the surface she may appear weak and fragile.

Of all my sisters, I think she's also the most damaged thru the complicated father and daughter relationship. She went thru many nasty and traumatic confrontations with my father in her teen years and even as an adult and was given way too many responsibilities very early on.

Money in our household was always a big reason for major conflicts, or rather, lack thereof was the reason for such fights. In mid 1980's, Moema started to date Alex when she was in her early 20s and the challenge was that Alex lived in a faraway city of Diamantina in Minas Gerais, about 15 hours from our hometown by bus which was the only mode of transportation we knew of with the exception of the return trip from the Amazon when we flew for the first time. They used to talk on the phone quite often and those conversations usually lasted a long time and ran up the phone bill to levels my father would completely lose his marbles over it. In one of those cycles of madness, my father came home from work late at night already a bit tipsy from his pit stop at the bar nearby for his liquor fix and he saw the phone bill on top of the TV where most of our bills would end up. He glanced thru it and was in complete discuss of the amount we were paying for out of state phone calls, and he started to threat and yell at Moema and Tata who were still living at home at that time and running up the phone bill.

"Yes, the bill is high, but Tata and I had been paying for it with the little money we are making from our jobs as manicure/pedicure and selling pies." Said Moema almost apologetically lowering her voice and looking down to avoid father's deep blue eyes.

"I don't give a fuck about your jobs and if you are paying these bills or not, the fact is, I work my ass off till late hours of the night seven days a week sometimes, and I have to pay expensive property taxes, put food on the table and pay all the other bills here and this is my house and in my house we don't run up phone bills to talk to boyfriends on the other side of the fucking country." Screamed my father in his usual end of the day tone of voice.

"But you don't have to pay the phone bills, I am sorry the bill has been high lately but that's the only way for me to talk to Alex." Replied Moema without raising her voice.

"I couldn't care less, why can't you find a boyfriend who lives nearby so they don't cost any money and you can help with the other bills instead?" Raising his voice even louder.

"I love Alex, he's my boyfriend and he happens to live in another state and the only way to speak with him is through the telephone and you should understand that." Moema replied louder and now almost challenging the king and his kingdom.

If there was one thing my father detested the most was being challenged by inferior beings (in his view). The veins around his neck started bulging and his bright blue eyes were getting bigger with that intense look of intimidation, fear and desperation which happened often. The tension was building up and I knew there would be only one outcome to this situation: violence/chaos.

He grabbed Moema by her right arm as if he was grabbing a fish still on the hook and throwing it into the boat before he hit it on the head with a baseball bat. He pushed her into the boy's bedroom, and he shut the door with such force that the entire house shook and all the glasses on windows and doors vibrated as if the familiar earthquake was upon us…and it was, earth was about to shake underneath all of us and each time it happened it only got intensified by the level of abuse and violence that ensued. The sound of those moments still lives inside me, and I am sure they still live inside my sisters. Inside the boy's bedroom resided a small table where our clothes would be ironed by my sisters and my stepmother. In fact, they would iron every item of my father's clothing, including his socks and underwear which, to this day I never understood the reason for such extreme care with his fucking socks and underwear, it made no sense to me but that's how he wanted and that's what he got it.

He was screaming and telling her not to talk back to him, not to challenge his authority and not to run up the fucking phone bill ever again and that he was going to teach her a lesson she would never forget. He yanked the electrical cord from the iron seating on the table inside the room and started whooping and beating her and screaming with so much rage that the entire neighborhood could hear and all we could do was beg for him to stop but nobody was brave enough or strong enough to stop him when he'd get to that level of insanity. My father was strong, forceful, and intimidating and when enraged, he seemed impossible to be stopped. There wasn't any opportunity to call the police those days because if there was, he would have been arrested and never let out of jail for all the insane violence he inflicted on us.

The bedroom door was close but not locked and my stepmother Nida would put all the kids under her arm, like birds do to protect their young chicks, and she would softly, thru the door, ask him:

"Zeze, please stop, you are scaring everyone and please don't hurt her, she's your daughter, please stop." Nida begged him to stop to no avail, often she would get his wrath too for interfering.

"They are not your daughters, and I am the one paying the bills here so don't get in the fucking middle of it." My father would scream back, and Nida would obey, and he would carry on with the only way he knew how to communicate with his kids, thru abuse, pain and violence.

That night something got into me, and I gathered enough strength and courage to open that door and when I saw him hitting and whooping her with the electric cord, which I had seen it too many times before, I jumped on his back and pushed him away. I was fifteen years old and not at all physically strong. I pushed him but he kept on hitting her as if I was just a fly that landed on his arm, and he swatted me away like I wasn't even there. His rage was so intense that he didn't even flinched at my effort to stop him and he kept with the screaming and the beating, slashing her legs, saying horrific things and putting so much fear on the rest of us that I am actually surprised that we all came out of that household and have all graduated from college, have pursuit successful careers in a variety of fields, from medicine, social worker to businessmen and have forgiven him and moved on to be socially, mentally, emotionally and psychologically well-adjusted human beings who help others and one another. It's a miracle none of us have ever been addicted to drugs or alcohol or have any vices.

I left out the loudest scream I could find in me, and I punched my father from behind on the side of his head with all my might and told him to let her go and beat me instead.

"C'mon, let her go, stop hitting her and hit me instead." I screamed in desperation with rage and enough courage found God knows where.

And the more I screamed the more he whooped that cord on her legs and anywhere on her body he could reach, as if he was possessed by the devil and nothing could stop him. I jumped on his back again and with a swift motion, hit him once more but this time on his face and without turning, he stopped at once.

Moema ran outside the bedroom crying, bleeding on her legs and arms from the strokes of that cowardly man, which during those days I wish was dead.

"You coward skinny shit. Don't you ever hit a man from behind again. Let me show you how you should do it!" He turned and charged towards me. I stood my ground, and we were now at each other's faces. God knows what might happen.

"Yes, you are right, I am the coward who hit a man from behind because another bigger, older and wanna be father is much more of a coward for hitting a girl, a woman, his own daughter, his own blood, his own kids, his wives and everyone else in between just because the fucking phone bill is too high or for some random bull shit reason. Go ahead, you fucking coward, take it out on me, I don't care anymore, hit me with the cord you have in your hands, slash my skin with your belt, cut me with the guava tree branch, brand me with the belt buckle like you have done so many times, punch me with your wrists and throw me in a garbage can if you want, but you will never hit my sisters again or another women in this house and if you do, I will fucking kill you...I will fucking kill you." I screamed with every ounce of energy I had left in me. "If you want to hit them, you are going to hit me first, in fact you are going to have to kill me first, but this will end here and I don't care what you do to me, go ahead, do what you do, hit me ass hole, what are you waiting for? HIT ME!!!!" I screamed and yelled my lungs out holding my tears inside in complete insanity, spraying my saliva all over his face and all over everything else, my mouth drooling, my neck veins dilating, my eyes about to pop out of its sockets...I turned into him, I am him... and if I have to, I'll kill this motherfucker, but this craziness has to stop.

I closed my eyes and I swear I felt the cord, the belt, the buckle, his wrists and all the other paraphernalia he used to torture and terrorize all of us all at once. I was dead as far as I was concerned. Suddenly, I couldn't hear a pin drop around, I couldn't see anything, as if I had gone into a different dimension...till the earthquake happened again and one of the windows shattered and came down waking me up from that nightmarish split second of a moment.

My father had left our bedroom, walked into his bedroom and he shut the door with such force that the cracked lamp cover from a misdirected ball from one of our many futebol games caved in and the glass splattered all over our living room. I remember snapping out of that moment completely spent, empty, hopeless, filled with fear and desperate for a different life, one without so much trauma, without so much fear and violence. I woke up from that moment to find Nida, Tata, Moema, Cesar, Sergio and Sandro, all crying, sobbing and in a state of complete disbelief and shocked seating in the living room floor while picking up the shattered glass all over the cold red and black cement tiles.

My father never came out of his bedroom for the rest of the night and was even more absent in the following weeks and months. He dove into work, drinking and the womanizing habits which stayed with him for a long time thereafter. I believe he didn't want to face or deal with any of us, especially me. He wasn't coming home for lunch which was a daily ritual in our household, and he wasn't speaking to anyone. He wouldn't even direct a look towards me, and I knew that night had a lasting effect on him, on me and in my entire family. Deep inside of me I was afraid I made things worse but had hopes that my intuition might be wrong and that the uncomfortable silence in our house might have been replaced with some peace and some much-needed changes and growth we all needed so we could move forward, especially my father whom I know never had anyone confronting and challenging him in such a manner.

A few months had passed, and although we continued to struggle with the silence treatment, my sisters started to think about moving to a place of their own, where they could have whatever phone bills they care to. They wanted to have their independency and free themselves of my father's rage and violence. The idea was noble, but the execution turned out to be a lot more difficult than anticipated.

They were looking for a place they could call their own with their own rules or lack thereof as far as they were concerned. But finding a place to rent was difficult because they didn't have transportation and they didn't want to live nearby our home for fear of my father's reaction and constant scrutiny. They also needed to stay close to the university because nobody had cars or rides to school. Rent was too high for the anemic and not at all stable income they earned by selling cakes and doing manicure/pedicure around town. They became frustrated and many different options were discussed, including moving to another state and living with some of our relatives, but that too proved to be challenging because of money, family ties and the fear of my father's retaliation which was a real thing.

They stuck around for two more years after that night, and it wasn't until I turned 17 that I heard they had found a place not too far from our house but far enough to create a buffer zone between my father and them. It was a small two-bedroom apartment in a humble building near our uncle Sebastiao, my father's older brother.

Moema and Tata were excited. I could hear them dreaming about the furniture they would eventually be able to decorate their place with, because in our house, only my father's furniture was allowed. Crazy dynamic and such a control freak he was that he wouldn't allow anything we wanted to purchase inside "his house" unless it was his idea.

I remember having to ask permission to buy two bunk beds with a little bonus I got at work from sunglasses sale my aunt Justina put me in charge of. I sold the glasses for more money than she had asked me to, and I kept the difference without telling her and on top of that she gave me a small bonus for a job well done. I took the entire amount and asked my sister Marina to help me buy two bunk beds for all of us boys because we were tired of our sleeping arrangement, and I was struggling with my height while sharing a bed with my younger brother Cesar.

My father didn't think we needed to buy the bunkbeds, but we bought them anyways. We asked our cousin Carlos next door to help us put them together and when my father came home from work one night, Marina showed him the new addition to our bedroom, and he couldn't care less, or at least that's how he reacted to it. Perhaps feeling inadequate for not being able to buy the bunkbeds himself or just simply stuck on his own egocentric, controlling and macho ways he had learned his entire life. He didn't react one way or another, he simply shrugged his shoulders and said:

"I am sure you overpaid for these shitty beds, they look flimsy and won't last like the other beds." He said with contempt and disregard for my effort.

He was right though; the old beds were there until the house was sold in 2020 during the Covid-19 pandemic and those beds went from the boy's bedroom to the girl's bedroom and outlasted all of us in that house. I guess there were so many challenges and obstacles and blood, sweat and tears experienced by those two single beds that not even bugs, pests and time wanted to deal with them.

There was something about my father which I was never able to understand: He wouldn't accept any ideas, any new furniture, any improvements, or changes in our house, even if the changes were for better and able to improve his own life. In one of those instances, I was sick and tired of seeing my father step on the toilet and do his business either standing or squatting on the toilet bowl leaving the edges all dirty from the dirt on the bottom of his shoes. He didn't even care to clean it after he left the bathroom, almost if he wanted us to clean it after him as in a sub-servant way of looking at his kids who were there to serve him exclusively. I decided to do something about it, and I knew the risk of a bigger price to pay besides the financial cost.

The mango season had been excellent, and I had made enough money to put a shower curtain around the square looking shower box we had in that single blue tiled bathroom in our house. I was also tired of having to wash the fucking bathroom walls from top to bottom everyday as part of my daily chores. I dreamt about getting out of the shower and not have to clean the toilet, mop the floor from all the water that splashed making the toilet, floor and walls all wet and dirty from soap scum, mud and mold, when all we really needed was a simple and inexpensive shower curtain like the ones I had seen at some of my relatives homes and I thought it was such a luxury and so fancy.

To install the shower curtain however, we needed to make some holes on the tile to screw a bracket for the PVC pipes where the shower curtains would hang from and enclose the two L shape sides of the squared shower box. The challenge was making any kind of holes in the walls and especially in the ugly blue tiles in that horrible bathroom was a major "no-no." My father would go berserk and would most likely break apart whatever we did because we didn't ask him. But if we ask him, he'd say a resounding "no" and all we were trying to do was make our lives better…go figure!

I had made a new friend with my new team at Joquei Clube whom his father owned a company that installed shower curtains and shower boxes around town, and I asked my friend Guilherme if his father could help me. I didn't consult with anyone because I knew my father wasn't going to approve of this idea and I didn't want anyone to be blamed for it besides me in case he'd go ape-shit crazy on us for making the bathroom better, drier and user friendly.

Guilherme talked to his father who agreed to come to our house to look at the job and give me an estimate. I told him I didn't have much money but if he could just help me make the holes in the tiles without cracking them, that would be great because I couldn't touch my father's tools and if I broke or cracked one of "HIS" tiles, all hell would break loose too.

Mr. Mendez came over on a Monday afternoon and after looking at the job, he told me that it would be much better to install a wraparound plexiglass shower box and door, change the medicine cabinet to match it and install a toilet cover on the toilet seat. I told him that was completely out of the question, and I didn't have enough money to do that and all I wanted was a shower curtain to stop water from splashing all over the bathroom. He told me that his son Guilherme had told him about me and that he had some remnants from another job and that I could pay him whenever and that any amount would be fine. He insisted and showed me the quality of the left-over material from a job he did uptown. He said he could do it all in just a few hours and cut it and install the tracks and the guides for the doors to run on and he could make everything very clean without cracking or breaking any of the king's tiles.

I wasn't sure if this was a good move because it would be a lot more permanent than what I had originally planned with the curtains and if my father decided to destroy it because it wasn't his idea, the original curtain I had planned was simple and inexpensive, and it would be easy for him to take it apart without having to break anything else, including my skinny bones.

Mr. Mendez said that my father would not destroy it because he was going to make it nice, and my father would appreciate the work and the quality of the material he was going to install.

"Trust me on this one Lenox, I understand your father and your concerns, but this will be so nice he will appreciate you for it." Mr. Mendez said confidently but he had no idea what the fuck he was talking about because I never told his son Guilherme about my father and his crazy ways of treating his children and how he controlled every little move in that wretched house.

Being a bit inconsequent and a risk taker at times, I agreed and told him that I would pay him for the entire job in installments because I was selling lots of mangos on weekends and he wouldn't lose any money. He told me not to worry and that it was his pleasure to finally meet me since his son, who was one year younger than me, admired how good of a defensive player I was and how fun it was to play with me and that he loved to watch me in practice.

"Wow, somebody likes to play with me and even watch how I practice?"

I replied surprised. Even my own family didn't have the time to watch me play or come to my practices.

Ok, I accepted his offer and crossed my fingers he could deliver the job without any problems and finish before my father came home in the evening, otherwise Mr. Mendez would run the risk of being killed alongside me.

Mr. Mendez finished the job on a timely fashion, and I decided to be the first one to take a long shower in that brand new shower box, seat on the toilet cover and organize the medicine cabinet with all my father's beloved Gillete razor blades perfectly in order from old to new before he came home.

I thought if the crazy man decides to break everything, at least I will know what it feels like to take a shower and not get the floors and everything else wet. If he breaks everything because it wasn't his idea, at least I got to enjoy it for a short moment, and I'd enjoy seating on the toilet with the plush cover without having to clean father's shoe marks all over it. I was happy for that moment in time and ready to accept whatever came after even if it meant my old man tearing it all down and whooping my skinny body in the process...which was very possible!

There was so much apprehension that evening with the expectation of my father coming home and walking into that bathroom and start screaming and destroying everything, I could hear the noises of the plexiglass being shattered and my father shouting and name calling running thru my head. My sisters and Nida loved the new bathroom and were so happy and surprised when they saw it that they hated the prospects of what that night could become for all of us. It was a huge deal and one that everyone was tense and uncertain about. What made me sad though was that we couldn't appreciate or enjoy anything that wasn't the king's idea, he rejected everything and controlled all of us.

He arrived late that evening and we were all seating in the living room watching some idiotic soap opera and all its rich characters who never seemed to have a job and all they do is argue and bicker about money and their love lives. We heard the vibration of the VW engine pulling into the garage and we were in pins and needles and couldn't even look at each other, tension was cutting thru the humid and hot air inside that house, and we just sat there and pretended we were watching television, but we were not, we were simply terrified of the prospects of what that moment might turn into. He walked thru the front door, and it was such a weird moment because this was supposed to be a good thing, but we were scared shitless with the prospect of what might happen.

He never really said hello or kiss his wife and kids when he came home, besides, that's too many of them and he's bushed and tired and probably smelled like cheap cologne, cachaça and old grease from the mechanic shop. He went straight into the bedroom, changed his clothes, and walked pass right in front of the television and into the bathroom which was to the left side of the living room while we were now looking at each other and just waiting for hell to break loose. He closed the door, locked the bolt by sticking his finger in the hole and pushing the hanging pin to the right and we heard the shower water running which meant one thing and one thing only: He opened the fucking shower box door to turn the shower on.

"Is he drunk and didn't notice the changes?" I asked Nida with a surprise and disbelief look in my face while my heart was beating out of my chest waiting for the noise of the plexiglass shattering on the bathroom floor.

"Shhhh, quiet please!" Said Nida putting the indicator finger over her mouth.

We were all looking at each other in complete disbelief and certain that something crazy was about to happen…we couldn't hear a pin drop except for the shower running.

My father never said a word about the new bathroom, he took his shower, used the toilet because we could hear the flushing of the water, he opened the medicine cabinet because his Johnson oil was inside the cabinet, and he used it every time after he washed his hair which was a daily habit. He never said a fucking word about it. He even learned how to seat on the toilet to do his business from that night forward because we never saw his blue eyes bulging thru the louver window again or his shoe bottom imprinted on the toilet seat.

I guess you can teach an old dog a new trick after all.

I was shocked and pleasantly surprised, we all were. From that night forward, I felt we could actually aspire to have a little hope and that was huge for all of us.

No compliments were ever given but none was expected, except for acceptance which, on it by itself, was more than enough given the level of fear and control we were under in that household.

CHAPTER XV
A Man In a White Cape

It was a muggy Saturday afternoon and my father had just got back from work. It was my sisters' D day, and an old moving truck was parked outside our front porch. Two men were waiting for orders from my sisters to start moving the furniture, but they had hit a roadblock. My father told them they were not taking any of the furniture from their bedroom which consisted of the two old single beds that were moved from the boy's bedroom to the girls after the bunkbeds acquisition, a termite infested wooden trunk that served as storage with a cracked mirror on top of it leaning against the wall, and an old falling apart dresser. These were things we wouldn't be needing anymore, and the girls were counting on because they had no other furniture in their new place.

"You decided to move, please go and never come back, but you are not going to take my furniture or anything else from this house except your clothes." Screamed my father in the usual loud tone of voice.

How cruel can a man be, really? Instead of encouraging his young adult daughters and helping them set up their new place, their new life and support them; he threatened and scared them and made this big rite of passage of moving out of your parent's house process, even more traumatic than it needed to be. But no surprises here, what else could we expect from our father? Well, a lot more actually!

Little did he know that I have been plotting my own move as well and that was going to take him by surprise. There was no chance of dialoguing with him and discussing the matter. I had to do it like I did with the bunkbeds, the shower and bathroom improvements, and so many other things around the house; do it and deal with his reaction and consequences later.

The writing was on the wall, this is going to be dramatic and traumatic all at once.

"Take one of the bunkbeds, I bought them with my own money, it will help you save space in your apartment." I said without any hesitation and fearlessly.

"But those are your bunkbeds and where are you boys going to sleep if we take them?" Replied Moema crying and disappointed my father wouldn't let them take their bedroom furniture, which was old, falling apart and about to become obsolete since they were moving out.

"Let's take the bunkbeds Moema, that's fine, the boys can use our beds to sleep, and they still have one bunkbed remaining." Said Tata with an attitude and a bounce on her step wanting to be out of there as quickly as possible.

He didn't argue with that because he knew I had purchased the bunkbeds with my own money. His way of agreeing with something he didn't agree with or couldn't control was just to remain silent and not show any type of emotion to it. I guess that worked in our favor sometimes, better than the alternative. The challenge with that kind of dialogue or lack thereof is that you can never be sure if what you are about to do is going to trigger a commotion because it wasn't verbally agreed upon. Oh well, fuck it.

During the last six months since I heard my sisters finalizing their plan to move out, I contacted a basketball coach at Corinthians Club, one of the most traditional and biggest futebol clubs in South America with the largest and most fanatic fan base in Brazil. They were putting a basketball team together and I knew of coach Mical, whom I had only seen on TV during the broadcasts of the Brazilian Basketball championship games. He had moved from Monte Libano Club to Corinthians and had put together a powerhouse of a team with a few National Team caliber players and couple of foreigners from Argentina and the U.S. forming a team that went on to win three Sao Paulo's state tiles, two national titles, one South America Championship title and a run to the semi-finals of the world club championship, a true powerhouse, and a legacy of a team.

A few weeks back I called the club and asked for the basketball office and to my surprise; Coach Mical picked up the phone and I froze when he said "hello!" I knew his raspy voice from the many TV interviews he's given. I didn't know what to say, my hands were sweaty, and I was shaking, and I wanted to hang up the phone and forget about all that business of me, yes me, trying to talk with one of the best basketball minds in Brazil at that time about a tryout? The familiar whining voice in my head was now getting louder and louder.

"Who the fuck you think you are Lenox?" That self-doubt voice in my head sounded very familiar, I muttered silently.

So many things going thru my mind in that split second with all the challenges I was going to have and being completely alone but the excitement, nervousness, anxiety, fear and feeling fucking lucky to have him on the phone at that particular moment pinched me,

"Wake the fuck up Lenox, this is your chance!!!" Screamed the other voice, "snap out of it motherfucker!"

"What do I tell him now?" I was hoping I was going to get his secretary or assistants on the phone and leave a nice message and feel like I gave it my best try because he would never call me back, they never do. But no, he picked up the phone and that phone call changed my life forever.

I told him a bit about myself and asked him if I could come and tryout for their Junior team and that I didn't have any expectation except that I was passionate about basketball and that I love the way he coached his Monte Libano teams, which in the year prior won everything from State's, National's and Club World Championship's.

He said that I could come and look for the junior coach and that he couldn't guarantee me anything except a place to stay for a few days with some of the Junior "futebol" players in the club's facilities behind the old practice stadium and eat with them during my stay.

"Say what?" I thought to myself. "That was too easy!"

I said yes, I would come, and I would find him and introduce myself once I got there and remind him of our conversation. He said he was a busy man and that wouldn't be necessary but he would leave a note for the junior's team coach with my information on it so he could arrange for my stay in their facility for a few days during the tryouts.

I also told him I didn't have any money except the bus ride ticket and that if I couldn't stay in the facility, I would have to sleep on the streets and I didn't know anyone else in Sao Paulo, a 20 million people megacity, and the 5th largest in the world. He told me not to worry and I could stay there for a few days.

When we were about to hang up the phone, I asked him if he could talk to my mother who wanted to speak with him. I handed the phone to my sister Marina who was the closest thing to my mom at that time of my life and still is to this day. I was afraid he would ask to speak with my father, and I wasn't about to let that dog out of the bag, as one could only imagine the scene…no fucking way!

I was now jaded and super excited, I couldn't sleep, eat, or think about anything else except how to tell my father and wonder how this news is going to be dealt with. I didn't tell anyone about it except my sister Marina. I kept it a secret because after all, the odds are completely stacked up against me and my father will make a mess out of this, no doubt.

He did…

As my sisters are now working with the two helpers grabbing their belongings and whatever else they could scrounge out of our house, I decided to break the news to my father but, I decided to tell him that I was going to move out and move in with my sisters into their new place and that, I thought would make an easier transition to moving out to another state as a minor barely 17 years old. I had this premonition that hell was about to fall on my head again.

Our entire family; Nida, Marina, Moema, Tata, Cesar, Sergio, Sandro, my father and I, we were all on the front porch under a tremendous amount of pressure and fearful for what my father might do because he was unpredictable at best and overly aggressive at worst when he didn't get his way in life, which he never did unfortunately.

"Dad, I am going to move with the girls to their new place." I said with very little confidence this piece of news was going to be taken well.

"Sure you are, under my dead body you are leaving!" He replied with his neck veins already bulging and his deep blue eyes looking devilish and scary as shit, as if he knew what was going on because I didn't have to repeat myself. Usually, people ask us to repeat something surprising to them or something they didn't expect to hear, like "what did you say? Or say it again!" Not my father though, this guy was always ready to attack the first time he heard anything and the only way he knew how; with fear, threats, violence and whatever else he'd come up with. Just like he expected us to obey his orders pronto, he also never asked us to say something he didn't like twice.

"I really want to move in with them father, I will miss them too much and I was hoping you would agree and help me make this happen, please?" I wasn't very firm, I was begging and wimpy and my father noticed I wasn't speaking with the same conviction I spoke that night I told him to stop hitting Moema.

"Listen Lenox, you are a minor and you are not going anywhere and that's the end of this discussion. YOU ARE NOT MOVING WITH THEM." He screamed for the entire neighborhood to hear and that was their cue to bring the fucking popcorn out because they were about to be entertained…again!

"Over my dead body, or yours!" He said and I didn't understand what he meant exactly and honestly, I was too tense, scared and nervous to hear and understand anything at that moment.

My aunt Laila, his sister who lived next door to our house and very familiar with our arguments and shouting matches came out and I could only see the top of her head walking on the sidewalk as the wall we had around our house was a bit too high for her short stature. Aunt Laila was a very calm and reasonable woman although I heard my cousins say all the hell she put them thru as well. No surprises there, she came from the same father and mother and was raised under the same roof with my crazy father. But knowing somebody else was coming to be with me and with us gave me some comfort. It reminded me of the car accident and how I was able to avoid being beaten and probably killed by having other people in the house.

"Dad, I am sorry, but this is not your choice, I don't want to live here anymore." I said confidently and with tears in my eyes and that was a big mistake. My father didn't respond well when the opposition showed fear and a sliver of weakness, he would pounce on it like a dog on a juicy bone and never let go.

"I already told you…you are not fucking going nowhere and if you try, I will fucking kill you, do you understand?" Replied my father with the usual rage and threats we were all so used to.

"Zeze, you are not going to kill anyone and Lenox, listen to your father, you are a minor and you can't leave unless he agrees to it, legally." My auntie Laila said with a very concerned look on her face.

"Lenox, listen to your father, please don't make things more complicated. Your sisters are already leaving, and this isn't easy on your father and it's not easy for anyone, please." Nida asked me with soft and submissive words.

"I don't understand it, why can't Moema and Tata departure not be a good thing for them, for us kids and for everyone else? Why can't they take the furniture in their bedroom, they don't have money to buy new ones and why they need to be punished? They are both in their 20s already, they are both going to university, have boyfriends, have jobs, and they are going to be living close to here and everyone else in this house will have more room, more food and more space to move around, what's so bad about that?" I asked in a loud tone of voice while drying my face from tears rolling down my cheeks.

"I am going with them, and you'll have to kill me then!" Turning to my father with conviction and courage this time around.

My father walked inside the house, went thru the front door which again was stuck on the bottom almost hitting him on his face as he tried to open it, slammed the front door shaking the foundation of our house, slammed his bedroom door so hard that everyone was jolted and spooked with the trembling of the guest room glass doors again which we had seen and heard so many times. I heard his heavy steps walking towards the porch and it gave me the creeps.

In the meantime, the two men helping my sisters were just about finished loading the few items they had to work with and ready to close the back gate of their truck and probably thinking; this has got to be the most fucked up family ever, but good soap-opera for sure.

My sisters were nervous because my dad disappeared inside the house and what does that mean? I was nervous and anxious because I probably screwed up their moving day by adding another layer of drama to an already very dramatic day. Nida was her old self, calm on the outside but scared shitless, bottom lips shaking and terrified inside, and the smaller kids were all seating there, not sure what the fuck was going on. Marina was trying to stay out of it, and it was probably a good idea because my father wasn't going to take any shit from anyone, and at that juncture, it was best to just let the dust settle and let things get calmer around our disjointed house. Aunt Laila was leaning against one of the pillars and when I looked at her, I noticed she was crying.

Just as my father was making his way back to the front porch with heavier than the usual heavy steps, I saw my cousin Hamilton, the police officer who also lived next door, walking home from work. He had his white civilian white shirt unbuttoned and flying on the wind as he usually liked to wear it when he was off duty from his policeman job. I could see his gun hanging on the side of his belt which would hold his baggy only pair of jeans he had. Hamilton was a quiet man, he had got into the civilian police squad a few years back and in one of our many conversations about his job, he told me that he had never used his gun and showed me the box of bullets he carried with him, which was still closed and sealed.

"Whenever I am called to do my job and I feel the need to use my gun or get into sticky situations, I walked away and do not get involved. My life is too precious, and my kids need me, I can't afford to take a bullet for people I don't even know, fuck that." He told me coldly.

I admired him for that. At first, I thought it was a bit chicken shit of him to not do the job he had signed up for, but I understood his reasons and I couldn't blame him. As someone who doesn't believe anyone should own a firearm or much less use one, hearing that from a police officer was very refreshing to me.

"Do you want to leave? Ok go ahead, you leave, and I will blow your brains on your way out!" Screamed my father pointing his loaded gun at my front lobe.

"What the fuck, are you serious?" I replied as he was pointing a gun to my head just about touching it.

My father was holding his 22 caliber Beretta pistol he kept inside the drawer of his bedside table directly onto my head. I had seen that gun before when he would bring it to our fishing trips and shoot snakes with it and he'd teach us how to use it but I never enjoyed the shooting lessons. I didn't like guns and had always felt very uncomfortable when someone had one around me. I feared guns and still do. I never owned a gun and never will.

Everyone was freaking out, aunt Laila begged my father to take the gun back inside the house.

"Zeze, you are my older brother, but you need to listen to me and put that gun away. You have all these small children here watching you and this is not good for anyone, please take that gun inside and put it away, I am begging you." She said crying and screaming at him this time.

My father didn't respond, in fact I don't think he even heard a single word she spoke. He was in his crazy "Zeze zone" I used to call it. When he got to that lonely zone/place, all noise and outside voices were blocked off and he just act on what he knew what to do well: inflict fear and pain if necessary to sooth his own.

I had seen my father draw a gun before. We were in Porto Velho and when the partnership with uncle Euripedes fell apart, he brought his faithful 22 out and threaten to kill my uncle and anybody else who got in the middle of it. When that happened, I didn't recognize my father. I knew he'd go radioactive at times, but the gun thing threw me off in Porto Velho and now he's threatening me, his own son, just because I want to leave in search of my own identity and my own space and away from this crazy fucked up place, I called home. What's a teenager to do?

Everything slowed down, it felt like a movie in slow motion and my cousin Hamilton was getting closer to our home now but like in a nightmare when you are about to die, he was too fucking slow and I could see that he was noticing the commotion and the yelling but never really got closer, it felt like. Besides, all the neighbors were on their own porch watching another episode of the best soap opera around: "The Jube's household dramas."

My brothers were crying, my sisters were crying and scared out of their minds, Nida was shaking like a bamboo stick on a windy day, auntie Laila was sobbing and begging him to stop, the two moving fellas were locked inside their truck watching the whole fucking thing and probably eating some popcorn and sipping on a cold beer and feeling like they got overpaid for this job and got more than what they've bargained for. Cousin Hamilton is walking in slow fucking motion into our porch and watching the very scene he always walks away from it: somebody with a gun in their hand about to commit a crime but his life is too precious and his kids need him too much for him to get involved…

"Ugh, you are fucked Lenox!" I thought my life was going to end but I felt that too many times before and perhaps this time was for real…I embraced the moment and rolled with it.

My father is out of his mind, and nothing is going to stop him, nothing, not even a police officer who never put bullets in his gun and had never even taken his gun out of its holster…what a clusterfuck I thought.

When I get to these situations, I don't panic, a different gear gets shifted inside of me and I think clearly and even though I was afraid my father might actually shoot me, I was defiant that perhaps this is what needed to happen for things to change around my house and in our lives. Maybe cousin Hamilton will put his never seen gunpowder gun to use for the first time and end this drama once and for all.

I had confronted my father before when he was beating Moema and this was easier because he wasn't hitting anyone and if he shot me, I figured he was so damn close to my head there was not chance he'd miss his target and I wouldn't feel anything. I would be dead in seconds and there's no pain when you are dead…those were my thoughts and I stuck with them. I was however worried for my brothers and how this might affect them. I was nervous for my sisters and feeling guilty because this was their D-day and now the focus was entirely on me, shit! So many feelings and so many thoughts in such a small amount of time and so many people affected by it.

"When does it ever end?" Maybe now…I felt this was the right time.

Nervously inside but with shaky confidence as in "fake it till you make it" kind of attitude, I turned to my father and unloaded my own ammunition.

"I am leaving and if you have to shoot me and kill me because I want to leave and get away from you and your fucking crazy and insane ways to treat your kids and wife, then go ahead and put an end to it. Do what you must do, but stop threatening me and everyone else, just pull the fucking trigger man! I will do what I must do and that is no longer your concern going forward. I do however have an idea for you though, after you shoot me, turn the fucking gun to your head and do us all a huge favor and pull the trigger again and die already, go to hell!" I started with a calm voice and ended screaming my lungs out.

I too was ape shit crazy come to think of it, but my thought was if am going to die, I might as well go out in style and take him with me.

King Zeze Jube's 22 caliber Beretta

I turn around and expected the worst, for the first time in my life I saw the image of my mother flashing in front of my eyes and, though I was occupied with the predicament I was faced with, I felt her presence and her angelic and soft smile as if she was trying to tell me something. Perhaps my father had already shot me, and I was dead already or about to turn "the lights off." I heard somewhere that when people are about to die their lives flash in front of them in a split second and life as we know it vanishes. Perhaps my life now was flashing and vanishing in front of me, and my mother was there to make me company and welcome me to the other side.

I felt a cold sensation on the side of my head as I am trying to make sense of all the images going thru my mind and when I turned, my father was holding his gun against my right temple, he cocked his 22 pistol and I realized he is not just going to shoot me, no siree... He is going to fucking blow and splash my brain matter in front of my entire family... what a scene, what a memory, what a last impression, what a guy huh!!!

"Pull the fucking trigger because if you don't pull the trigger I will leave anyways and I will never see or speak to you again and I will be dead to you anyways. C'MON, PULL THE FUCKING TRIGGER!" I screamed for the entire neighborhood, truck drivers, and passing byers audience to hear me, feeling the blood gushing thru my face and veins, my heart beating out of control and watching my entire family witness this moment in time which forever will change the direction of our lives.

Cousin Hamilton and Aunt Laila yelled at him not to pull the trigger and to move the gun away.

"Brother...Zeze, please put the gun away, I beg you. This is your own son and Lenox is not going anywhere, he's not going anywhere, and you have my word...please put the gun away, I implore you." Sobbing and begging her brother on her knees. Aunt Laila kept on repeating over and over again for him to put the gun away to no avail.

Cousin Hamilton: "Uncle, you must put the gun away from his head or I will have to do something about that."

Poor cousin Hamilton, the fucking guy runs away from these types of scenarios every day to preserve his life and the livelihood of his children and now, he may have to draw his gun and finally put it to use against his own uncle, what a clusterfuck!

I knew Cousin Hamilton didn't have any bullets on his gun though, I knew that because the box of bullets was sealed last time he showed it to me and he never used his gun at work. What are the odds he will have to use it now, on his own uncle and he had no bullets in it?

"Motherfucker!!!"

Cousin Hamilton (Right)

My father put the gun down and he walked away into his bedroom but this time there was no slamming of doors or screaming of any kind. He simply walked away, walked thru the living room and into his bedroom, fell onto his small double size bed and I was waiting for the noise of that gun to go off on his own head. I had no doubt that the only way out of such embarrassing and traumatic situation, was for him to take his own life so he wouldn't have to deal with me or any of us ever again.

"God damn it, he might as well come back here and just shoot me because I will never forgive myself if that gun goes off inside his bedroom." My mind was spinning and I was sure he was going to do it and I had no doubt this was the only outcome…he was going to blow his own brains out.

A sharp booming noise went off and we all jumped in desperation only to realize one of the old neighbor's Vespa without its muffler just passed by in that noisy corner spooking all of us…what a fucking day, what a fucking timing!

His gun never went off in his bedroom and I am thankful and grateful for my father not shooting me and specially for not killing himself for I don't know how this story would ever be written had that happened.

Nida went inside the house and into the bedroom and I don't know what they talked about or if they even talked about anything, but she was there with him and she stayed there for as long as I can remember afterwards. I am so thankful for Nida, for my cousin Hamilton who probably was sent by God with his unloaded gun because without a doubt he was at the right place at the right time and most importantly, he didn't have to use his bullet less gun on my father. I was grateful for my brothers and sisters who made it so difficult for my father to pull the trigger in front of them and hopeful we would be able to live thru this trauma and get to a better place in life eventually.

I am also indebted to my mother who appeared to me in a moment of despair, and I believe embodied my aunt Laila's body and begged my father not to kill the child she went thru so much to give my father the boy he desired, the son she sacrificed her health and ultimately her life for to make my father whole. Thanks mom!!!

Aunt Laila sat down next to me, put her left arm around me and whispered in my ears: "Don't go anywhere, wait till you turn eighteen and then you can do whatever you want but promise me you won't go anywhere."

My father and his sister aunt Laila

"Alright. I won't, thanks." I said coldly and numbed.

Moema and Tata got inside the moving truck and left crying and in complete shock, my brothers went inside the house to watch Tom & Jerry, Marina turned on the TV for them. Nida was still inside the bedroom with my father, cousin Hamilton walked away with the wind blowing his white cape looking shirt, like a cowboy with his gun still in the holster, yet to be drawn. Aunt Laila walked home next door, slowly and limping from spending too much time on her bad knees and drained from allowing my mother to use her body as a conduit.

I sat there in between the two pillars that hold the porch up, the same two pillars that made me company in that car crash Sunday afternoon. I didn't have any feelings; I couldn't cry or talk. I was empty and nothing made any sense anymore. The only think I could think of was how beautiful my mother was and how little time I had with her.

Two pillars and Lenox

Perhaps we need more of these heavy dramas around here so she can come back more often and spend a little more time with me. I miss my mom; I miss her dearly and I hope I will get to see her again one day in different circumstances!!!

I didn't know where Marina was, so I peeked thru the cracked glass living room door and I could see her, seating on the torn up leather and mahogany seat in front of her old Essenfelder piano, with her eyes shut, her mouth trembling, her head tilted to the right, tears falling on the ivory black and white keys and probably gathering strength to move on.

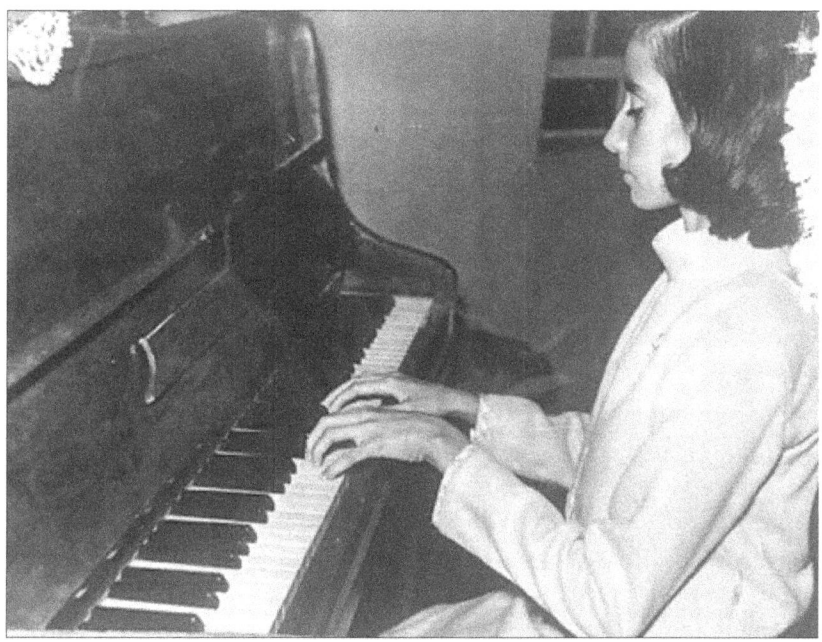

Marina & Essenfelder Piano

"How to move on from this?" I thought.

Still, I felt nothing. I laid on my back on the cold red cement floor of our porch and felt the familiar comfort of the Carnauba red wax we used to treat the entire house tile and cement floors with, specially the "alpendre" and garage. The cold temperature of that flooring which, often scrapped and scuffled my knees while washing it and waxing to my father's liking was now a comfortable place to be. Often, I would lay down on it and allow it to cool me off from the hot and muggy days in that morbid city and especially from the heated fights and furniture throwing I witnessed so many times in my house. Suddenly, I heard a distant sound, but I couldn't identify what it was at first after such exhausting chain of events. Maybe I am sleeping and this whole thing was just another nightmare, and I am waking up from it? But it wasn't, as much as I wanted it to be just that, just a bad dream, a nightmare. No, this was real, it happened, and we must find ways to heal, to forgive and move on someway, somehow. These events were and are strong reminders of the type of life I want to live and how I want to treat my own kids and the people I love the most. Events that will stay with me forever, that defined who I wanted to be as a man, shaped me as a human being, soften me as a father and helped me understand other people's pain and suffering.

Yet, that distant sound was familiar, it had this beautiful melody, and it was soft, soulful, and extremely sad. I realized my sister Marina was playing "Le Lac De Come" by Giselle Galos. A song she would play occasionally when her students asked her to play something for them, or when we had important visitors and my father demanded Marina to play it for our guests. A song that, to this day melts my heart when I hear it and brings back so many memories; good and bad ones, but mostly important ones which allows me to revisit those days and have mercy, compassion, and love for my father. A song that reminds me that we are all flawed people doing our best to overcome our struggles and our shortfalls.

In that moment I chose to believe that my father loved me so much that he was willing to kill me before he let me go. I figured the only way to move forward was to forgive and believe in love instead of hatred and resentment. I Knew then I wasn't having a nightmare, and I broke down, I cried, I sobbed, and I was now laying in a pool of my own salty and warm tears wishing for my mother to appear once again so I could stroke her cold and comfortable upper arms with the back of my hand while staring at the ceiling and feeling her love, her sweet and kind motherly love.

To quote one of my favorite American memoirists and poet.

"History, despite its wrenching pain, cannot be unlived, but if faced with courage, need not be lived again."

Maya Angelou

Fim

www.ingramcontent.com/pod-product-compliance
Lightning Source LLC
Chambersburg PA
CBHW051146120626
46547CB00012B/962